Lillie peae

2007

F ll the Best .

LEGENDS
OF AN OLE'
LINEMAN

[signature]

LEGENDS
OF AN OLE'
LINEMAN

TRUE LESSONS AND LEARNING FOR A JOURNEYMAN

DANNY L. RAINES CUSP

XULON ELITE

Xulon Press Elite
2301 Lucien Way #415
Maitland, FL 32751
407.339.4217
www.xulonpress.com

© 2022 by Danny L. Raines cusp

Paperback ISBN-13: 978-1-66286-398-1
Ebook ISBN-13: 978-1-66286-399-8

FORWARD

I was 18 and about to graduate high school. My Dad had informed me that I needed to start looking for a job. It was either go to college, which my family could not afford, or work. I applied for employment at Bell South and Georgia Power. That seemed to be the direction I wanted to go. It was a natural fit after my summer job at Macon TV Cable as a Service Installer between my junior and senior years of high school. I did much of the work off a ladder, but I was forced to climb poles in some locations. I will never forget the day I was handed a set of hooks and a body belt and safety, walked over to a pole in the yard at the storeroom off Broadway in Macon. I was told, "Here is a pole. There are your tools". He demonstrated climbing one time. I took a set of climbing tools home and practiced on a pole in my front yard. Looking back, I went to work with absolutely no idea of the dangers of climbing and fall accidents.

I was 17 years old in 1965. I do remember climbing a pole on Wimbish Road to connect a TV Cable drop up to the main cable, and the NESC specifications space was off; there was hardly any space between Supply and Communications, much less the now required 40". I was watching my feet climbing and stopped when I bumped my hard hat on the bottom of a transformer. I looked up and realized what I had done, and my heart dropped to my socks. I call it "University of Hard Knocks" learning. Again, that could have been much worse, but I was blessed. I worked at Macon TV Cable that summer and had many learning experiences. Those lessons planted a seed of yearning to know more about utilities. That job only lasted a few weeks, and I returned to school. Bob Bonifay was the Manager of Macon TV Cable, which Cox Cable now owns. It was a great experience I and made pretty good money for a high school kid. Brannon Bonifay, Bob's Son, was the quarterback for my high school football team, the Lanier Poets. I was a linebacker until my own teammate tackled me after I made an interception in a scrimmage game and blew my right knee up. Small world. I completed my senior year and started looking for a job in the utility industry.

Now, after forty Years with Georgia Power and fifteen as a Consultant and Trainer, I want to present a book containing a series of short stories and tales that need to be told before I forget most of them. Thanks to many that shared some of their most fond memories so I could include them in this book. Please. Enjoy the stories. They are real. Ken Wall, Ernie Campbell, Bob Rogers, Robert Wix, Doug Colquitt, and others contributed to these stories. Looking back, I'm so glad I made the decision for that job all those years ago. It was the start of a long, fulfilling career that gave me great experiences and memories.

HOW IT BEGAN

Two months before graduating high school, I started job hunting and applied for positions at Bell South and Georgia Power Company. I interviewed with both companies, but Georgia Power had always been where I wanted to be. I considered both jobs, but I had an uncle who advised me that there would always be a need for someone to get the lights on for everyone. Even back then, my uncle visualized that technology would soon change the landscape for communications and power companies. I was looking for a challenging job: something permanent and satisfying, with a future. An accident I witnessed when I was just a kid also contributed to my interest. A neighbor was installing an outside TV Antenna on a metal pole. He lost control and dropped in on an energized 4kV primary. Two men were injured badly. Witnessing the accident with all the fireworks sparked my interest, so I started down a path to seek more understanding of just what happened. I was fascinated that something could be that powerful, yet still controlled. I wanted to know more about how someone could work around and touch electrical equipment and not be injured like those two men.

Now, I had an opportunity to work with Georgia Power as a Helper on a Line Crew. My career path had been determined. I had a final interview for the position with Jess Green at the old GPC Division Office, in Macon, Georgia. I passed the Mechanical Aptitude Test and was awarded the helper job on Jay Walker's Line Crew. I will never forget what Jess told me on June 6, 1967: "Bring a biscuit for lunch and be at the 'hole' at 7:30 Monday morning". The starting pay was $2.08 per hour, with a promised negotiated Union Contract guaranteed raise

1

on July 1st of $.10 per hour. I was in "hog heaven" and making a decent wage for that time. The door of opportunity opened, and I never looked back on anything else. I completed 40 years and six months of service filled with opportunities and worked with some of the best people in the world. I loved every minute of it and still do.

EARLY DAYS

There were no development plans and no OSHA Rules. All Georgia Power's Safety Rules were found in a book called Section "0". It was all we had, along with the experience of some of the best linemen in the business. Section "0" was the name of the Safety Manual for Georgia Power. I asked how Section "0" came to be. The story was, that in 1926 when Georgia Power started as a company, it was documented that 50 % of line workers never made it to retirement, if they stayed in the business. So, a basic set of rules for safe worker practices was written and was to be added to the company policy. There was discussion about referencing the rules because they were important to line workers. The suggestion was made to put Section "0" in the construction manual called the Specifications Book. The first chapter was named "Overhead Line Construction", so the "Safety First" theory hit a bump in road with the name. The decision was made. It was to be called Safety and designated as Section 1. Still, the company did not want to change the entire outline of Construction Standards, so the Safety Manual was Called Section "0" and placed in front of Overhead Line Construction. The safety rules should always be the first consideration in the Construction Manual. Section 0 was later rewritten and edited. As time went on, the industry changed, and it is now a separate small safety manual that reflects the basics of the OSHA Construction and Maintenance Standard. It is a small, pocket-sized book that is still in print after eleven edits. The document is now a negotiated set of safety rules that the company and IBEW LU 84 review together when needed. Both parties agree on the safest methods to perform the line work, while meeting or exceeding OSHA Standards. So, when accidents happen and investigations occur, the accident committee uses not only OSHA standards as a foundation, but Section "0" is also used and referred to. If the company safety rules are violated, the workers are also viewed as violating agreed Labor union rules. The fact that the union and the company sign the safety manual, like a contract, creates "ownership" of the safety program and the safety rules by all employees.

The "Hole" on Riverside Dr.

Carl Funderburk was the District Superintendent in Macon when I started with Georgia Power. He was a nice guy, but I never got to know him well. We all stayed in the "hole", while he and the office staff were upstairs. Carl would show up on jobs with Lee Saunders to visit crews occasionally. If we had a large storm or a "special occasion", he would come out of his shirt and tie and put jeans and boots on (to mostly sit in the office).

Lee Saunders was a great guy. He would visit often, and he had a favorite saying about Safety Rules. He always said, "as long as your butt is round and brown and pointing to the ground, you better do… (he would fill in the blank)." Lee lived near the Key Street office off Burton Avenue. He always had a green vehicle to drive; you could see him coming from a mile away. One Monday morning, the green Chevrolet he drove was sitting in the garage on Key Street, destroyed. Someone had lost control of their vehicle and hit Lee's car while it was parked in front of his house. Now, that started an interesting conversation! Lee was there for a long time after our move from the Riverside Drive office to Key Street Operating. I am still friends with his daughter now, many years later.

John Lane was "South Macon Power and Light", and he was the most unique lineman I ever worked with. John taught me a lot, and he will be mentioned many times in this book. When I was on the Southside Cut-In Truck with John, we would work like crazy to get new services installed, rewires tapped up, and services ran in the early mornings; then, we would stop at Hard Rock Grill in the afternoon to have a cup of coffee in the winter or a cold drink in the summer. John was also the person that got me involved in bowling. We had fun in the bowling leagues at Shurling Drive and later, at Northside Bowling Center, where I met Vicki Dartez (now Raines), the lady I have been married to for 40+ years. We all traveled around to the State, Southeast, and National Bowling Tournaments for years. I never was a "Pro Bowler", but I carried a consistent average of about 185-190 yearly.

Carl was promoted to Vice president of the old Valdosta Division before the company was restructured into regions. After Carl left, Ed "Doodle" Grubb showed up as Superintendent just before we moved off to the Key Street office. Doodle was one of the most popular superintendents we ever had. On a hot summer night, I saw him load transformers (into what was then an appliance delivery truck) and deliver them to crews, because there were so many trouble calls and not enough help. He would jump in with crews, changing out burned-up transformers and work to get the lights on. Things like this made him one of the most respected superintendents there was. All the employees appreciated him and his work ethic. His nickname, "Doodle", came from him sitting at school (and later staff meetings), doodling pictures on notepads. One of the most repeated statements Doodle made was," if a company had good management, there would be no need for Unions". Georgia was an "Open Shop" Right to Work State. IBEW 84-896 was in Macon at the time. You could join or not and still receive the same working conditions and benefits. I was a member until I was promoted to Supervisor in the mid-'80s. It was customary to withdraw from the Union during a promotion to a "management" position.

Buck White was the Supervisor of the meter shop then. His son, Chuck, was a GPC employee with whom I became good friends. We both successfully got promotions to Jonesboro Noah's Ark Operating. I was a Crew Foreman, and Chuck was in Engineering and Marketing Sales. We bowled in leagues together in Conyers, Georgia. Our wives remained friends, even today, some 30 years later.

Evelyn Trisler was the Secretary/Operating Assistant on Riverside Drive; she was the "Mother Hen" and go-to person for almost anything in the front office. Ms. Evelyn had a large jar of marbles on her desk that she kept as souvenirs and memories from the Trouble men and the Cut-In and Out-Linemen. Anytime we were in the field working and found marbles while digging, we would take them to her for safe keeping. She loved the cats eye marbles the most. Ms. Evelyn recorded all our time sheets and took care of all the medical records, also. John Powell was the District Engineer back in those days. "Long John" would always be sitting across from Ms. Evelyn with his feet propped up on the desk. It was always a sight to see because Ms. Evelyn was not happy with shoes being on desks.

Many executives came through Riverside Drive Operating on their way "up the ladder". Garnett Grubb and Mike Garrett are two. Mike went on to be the President and CEO. Like most of us, Garnett ended up at 241 Ralph McGill and held several different marketing and sales positions. Both are retired now. Mike lives east of me on a farm in the country. He came from a Dublin farm, so he bought a nice tractor and is now back "home" again on the farm. Garnett and his lovely wife, Peggy, live a few miles south of me near Forsyth, Georgia.

Many of the employees in Macon would eventually end up working in the corporate office on Peachtree Street, and later at 241 Ralph McGill Blvd. I wound up on the 18th floor as the Safety Consultant. The elevator could be taken to the 23rd floor, but you still had one set of stairs to climb in order to get to Mike Garrett's office. The "Leaning Tower of Power" was what the Corporate Office was referred to because of the design of the building. It sits almost empty today, after COVID. Before I retired, it had 2000 + employees in and out of the doors daily.

All the Vice Presidents I ever worked for were great friends, but some early on were a little rough around the edges. I will never forget Red Roberts and how he introduced himself at the first safety meeting we attended together. We had one every month. Lee Saunders or one of the supervisors would present the topic. "Red GD Roberts" was what I heard him refer to himself as during introductions. I thought to myself, "I do not want to make him mad for any reason". A lot has changed in leadership styles since the late sixties. Mr. Roberts once stated he did not want anyone from Atlanta in "his" division, if they were not invited. Anyone from Atlanta was welcome to come through the Macon Division, but not stay. This practice was referred to as "empire building" back in those days. And the Macon Division started in Jonesboro District and ended in Kingsland, Ga. A very large piece of Geography.

FIRST LINE CREW

As I mentioned, I started as a Helper on Jay Walker's Line Crew, working out of the "hole" on Riverside Drive in Macon, Georgia. Bobby Waller, Ronnie Spillers, and Wayne Fountain were the three linemen, Mike Tucker was the Apprentice, A. E. "Barney" Register was the permanent Winch Truck Operator, and I was the "Grunt" Helper. It was a great group of guys and I sure learned a lot from them.

Ronnie Spillers took me up on my first General Aviation flight in 1968. We flew out of Middle Georgia Regional Airport in a plane Ronnie owned. We would go to the airport after working all day at GPC and work on, wash, or clean the aircraft. We would then go up for short flights around Macon. Twenty years later, I took flying lessons and earned my private pilot's license and fly out of Macon, renting airplanes from Lowe Aviation. I never considered flying as a career at only 19 years old, but I should have. By the time I got my license, it was too late to even think about a career in flying, but I might have had I started flying earlier. Ronnie Spillers is now a retired Baptist Minister, still living near me in Georgia. I spend most of my time flying on Delta, Still go up in general aviation occasionally.

Jay Walker's crew worked overhead, primarily Distribution. I stayed on Jay's crew for a year or so until I had the tenure to be a Winch Truck Operator. In those days, it was simply "time in" seniority that got you promoted to the next classification. There was a significant pay increase from Helper to Winch Truck Operator, a small one to Apprentice Linemen, and another significant pay increase to Lineman. There were several different steps with small increases within each classification as well. Even back then, it usually took about four years to get from Helper to Journeyman Lineman. "Learn as you go" was the name of the game. Promotions came around by someone above you on the seniority list transferring, being promoted, or retiring. There were long spells that you stayed at the same classification. The only raises during these spells were the incremental step of $.10 or $.15 per hour within the pay grade classification. A WTO had about six steps, unless one wanted to be a "Permanent" WTO, choosing to not continue to Apprentice or Lineman. A Permanent WTO job was at or slightly above the Apprentice pay. Pole climbing, fear of heights, or just not wanting to put their hands on hot primary were some reasons for staying back and not taking promotions when the time came. I always thought a Permanent WTO was an asset to the company because they took better care of their equipment. The IBEW negotiated all the steps and pay grades for the employees. I joined IBEW LU 84-896 as soon as I was a permanent employee.

After a brief time as a Helper, my next step was Winch Truck Operator. I successfully bid on a Truck Driver position on a three-man crew. Three-man crews worked both Underground and Over Head jobs. I was introduced to Direct Buried UD Cable Installation and Maintenance and worked on Three Man Crew for about a year and a half. It was a great learning opportunity to work with two very experienced linemen, Earnest Mooney and Johnny Brasselle. Those guys taught me so much throughout my time with them. There were many other linemen on crews that I worked with: George McCleskey, Jimmy McDaniel, John Lane, Bennie Britt, Bill Hammock, Sidney Boyd, and many others that I will mention in the stories.

In those days, new employees were hired as "petty cash" with no benefits until they were permanent employees. There was a six-month probation period for newly hired employees. The company evaluated new employees to be sure they would make it on a line crew and to see if they wanted to stay in the business long-term. Not all were cut out for the work: outside in cold and hot weather, working all hours of day and night, and incredibly long hours restoring power after storms. I can remember working 24-48 hours straight many times. It was tough even for a young man. I can now understand why there are limitations for driving a Commercial Motor Vehicle after being on duty for so long. It is like being under the influence of drugs or alcohol. I have driven to motels after working for 36 hours or more and cannot remember the drive. I would wake up and not know where I was or how I got there. Looking back, it is kind of scary when you think about the tasks we were working on while being that tired. Hence, "hours of service" are important in today's world.

The summer of 67' was hot as blazes. All employees were evaluated for fitness for at least every three months and on probation until they were made permanent employees. During probation, if you missed a day, your seniority/start date would start back on the day you returned. I overheated and was out sick for three weeks at the end of June until I recovered from heat exhaustion. I returned on July 1st, so my seniority date then became 7/1/1967. Chappie Vaughn and Wesley Mosley were hired after me, but "jumped me" in Seniority because of those missed days. Because of this, they made Lineman ahead of me. I hated that for years. The IBEW filed a grievance and fought that policy, eventually winning the battle, so the start date would remain the same. July 1st was the beginning of contract negotiations between the Company and IBEW for wages, benefits, and working conditions. The policy was changed that year, but I never got those three weeks back. I will never forget that. My actual start date was June 5th, 1967. That one sickness cost me a lot of money over my career because of that rule.

One of the first memories I have as a Helper on Jay Walker's Line crew was the time the crew was working in Wayside, Georgia, changing out rotten poles that had been found while performing inspections. Wayside was 8-10 miles northeast of Gray and about 25 miles east of Macon. The old VHF radios would just barely reach out to that part of the district, and we had no telephones in those days. The crew stopped for lunch, and I had a corned beef hash sandwich in my lunch box. I ate the sandwich for lunch and by 1:15 PM, I was as sick as I have ever been. The crew recognized that I was sick and needed to get to the hospital, after I passed out. They put me in a bucket truck and headed to Macon. They called the dispatcher, had an ambulance meet the bucket truck on Gray Highway (about halfway to Macon), and transferred me to the ambulance. I was still unconscious. When we got to the Emergency Room, I woke up long enough to remember the doctor asking me if I had been drinking moonshine. "No" was my answer. That's the last thing I remember until about midnight that night. I then found out that I had a severe case of food poisoning. Mom and Dad had milder cases but did not require medical help. I stayed on IVs until the next day and was released from the hospital. It turned out the can was damaged; it had a dent that no one saw, causing the meat to spoil. I do not eat corned beef today and that was over 50 years ago. Thanks to my crew members, I survived. I think that Wayne Fountain drove the bucket to meet the ambulance.

Different Jobs

There were other positions such as Cable Splicer jobs, like Cecil Brown worked on Network UD with Paper Insulated Lead Cable. I had my first taste of Paper Insulated Lead Cable Network primary systems working with Cecil Brown converting a Spot Network to UD Transformers for an addition to the then Macon Hospital (now Navicent Medical Center of Central Georgia). I soon found out I did not care for Network UD. I boiled a little oil, helped wrap a few splices, and spent much time pumping water out of manholes in downtown Macon. There was and still is a network of primary and secondary for multiple square blocks downtown that the two three-man Network crews took care of. I filled in when someone was out as a WTO. Ernie Campbell, Bennie Arnold, and Dallas "Chick" Ethridge eventually became the splicers after Cecil Brown was awarded a Line Supervisor job. Those were great opportunities for those who chose not to be linemen. Chick Etheridge eventually landed a Tool Specialist position at Key Street. Chick could repair anything from a hot stick to a set of chain hoists. Also, I remember Chick was on the way to work one morning and passed a Kidney Stone and ran off I-16 and had to be picked up and taken to the hospital. Another Ethridge was Skeet Ethridge, Chick's cousin who worked with GPC for several years. Skeet left the company and got a job at Warner Robins AFB. Skeet was a Lineman that could plan a job as well as anyone. Smooth on a pole. Taught me many things. Chick also worked closely with Luther Harrison. Luther tested all of our rubber gloves and blankets. We would sometimes help Luther move stuff around, especially on rainy days when outside work was slow unless there was trouble. Luther was a very quiet person and never said a lot, but when he did, you need to listen. Luther also offered great advice to all the young guys.

WILD AND CRAZY

I t is a wonder that everyone was not fired back in those days. We could never meet today's "standards" with the behaviors and language everyone used back then. I will share a few examples. When an employee was going to get married, they were painted with locating paint or transformer Pad Mount Green. I will not go into many details on where this paint was applied, but this caused heartache for many. I heard that one fiancé was so upset, that she postponed the wedding due to the paint. I also remember a specific lineman who was to be married for the second time that told us, "no one is brave enough to pin me down and paint me". So, the group decided that we would shave off his mustache. That decision started the battle. We had some mighty men in those days. We did catch him after a chase through the business and engineering office, out the front door, to the road going up Rose Hill Cemetery, next door to the "hole" on Riverside Drive. When we caught him, we shaved off the right side of his mustache. So, in the end, he was correct when he said we would not paint him. He had to finish the job at home; how crazy were we?

Another tradition was having to buy everyone beer on the last day on the job before a promotion to a new position. As you can imagine, that caused much grief. When the office was on Riverside Drive, the road to Rose Hill Cemetery or the employee parking lot near the garage was a short walk from the locker room. When the GPC office moved to a new location on Key Street, the employees would gather in the employee parking lot and have beer iced down for the celebration on the last day of the old job. Everyone participating would meet in the parking lot and have a beer or two, sometimes one too many. It sometimes got too loud, and a few would leave the parking lot and go to the nearest bar to finish the celebration. This same type of "celebration" would occur on Union meeting nights. There were a few that tried to drink all the beer that was brewed the day before and wound up in trouble. A specific lineman attempted to drive out of the Key Street parking lot, ran over a gate post, and caused damage to the 30-foot-wide double gate and to the fence. At a different Union meeting, another employee had too much to drink; he went out of the hall to Holt Ave, stole a dump truck, rode around town in it, and was later arrested for vehicle theft and DUI. It was different in those days. Things like this could happen and it all was okay. Fines were paid and everyone returned to work. I was not there for either of these events; I had already left and gone home. I was only a Young WTO or an Apprentice when these things happened. Glad I was not a witness! Those were the days….and there were many more fun stories, but not in this book. On hot days back then, during lunch on Friday, a junior person on the crew would take money collected and go to the store to buy beer for an "afternoon break". It was just a way of life back in those days. I am genuinely amazed that more incidents didn't happen.

HELPER DUTIES

As a Helper on a line crew, my job started every day by icing the water keg and cleaning off the material trailer from the day before. The crew rarely got in early enough to properly clean and restock the material trailer with all the "minor materials", like bolts, 2X2 and 4X4 washers, lock nuts, poly wire, copper tie wire, or guy wire. The pay-out reel for the guy wire back then was an old car tire from the garage. We would put the guy in the tire and then cut the bands to release the coil. I remember that some guys would cut the 10 M guy wire with their 9" Kline cutting pliers. After that, the material for that job would be ready to load. Then, we would go to the transformer rack to load transformers, and finally, go to the pole pile to load poles.

One of the first big jobs working on Jay Walker's crew was a line extension off Hwy 247 in Macon, near the airport. I was introduced to my new "kinfolk", fondly called a "cutting cousin". It was a tool to dig a hole for an expandable bust anchor. It had an extendable handle, to allow one to get a down guy anchor hole about 8' deep. The correct starting position was a 45-degree angle to the pole, with a guy installing the guy rod. I was taught never to install the guy rod straight down, which was the easiest way to start, or the pole would be lost in a strain until the guy caught up with the angle. I still see young apprentices today installing anchors at incorrect angles. You take pride in your work when after the conductor is pulled to correct tension and you go back years later and see the pole in the same shape as the day the conductor sagged. Linemen are one of the few occupations that allows a person to ride up and down the road and see their work. This fact instills pride for linemen everywhere across this country.

We had two line supervisors back then. The crew foremen reported direct to the line supervisor, J. C. Edwards. Mr. Edwards was better known as "Sarge" because everyone thought he acted like a Drill Sergeant in the Army. He was honest, straight forward, and had zero sense of humor. J.C. was once shot at by bank robbers at 1st National Bank in Westgate Mall. He shouted on the company radio, "They are shooting at me!". Jim Lunsford was the service supervisor over troublemen, UD Crews and Cut in Crews. He was soft-spoken and one of the nicest guys I met when I went to work at GPC. I thought the world of him because he was such a nice guy. I lost track of both of these guys and have not heard anything from anyone about them in years.

The first PPE I was given was an old, smooth top "turtle shell" hard hat. GPC had been in hard hats for about three years when I started. I wish I still had that old hard hat now. It would undoubtedly be a keepsake. I will never forget the day I stopped at the Piggly Wiggly on my way home to pick up items at the grocery; As I walked down the aisle, I saw a hard hat going the opposite direction on the next aisle. Chick Ethridge was so proud of his hard hat and was so proud to work at GPC, that he wore it home every day. We were all proud. GPC was one of the first investor-owned utilities to wear hard hats in 64' after the Edison Electric Institute completed a research project and determined that head injuries were one of the most common injuries in the industry. If you look at the OSHA Act of 1970, 29 CFR 1926.100 was the first working standard passed, requiring hard hats in construction activities. A direct result of the feedback from the Edison Electric Institute.

Another story comes to mind about Chick. When the office was on Riverside Drive, we had many rainy days. The loading dock was not completely covered, and it wasn't easy to clean and restock the trucks. Chick was the truck driver on one of the first Red Corner Mount Digger Derricks we had. There were old "A" frame line trucks, some were yellow or red, until GPC finally went to all white trucks. When

Chick was assigned this new Corner Mount, he would take this beautiful red line truck to the mechanic's garage next door. He would find an empty bay, wash it, and was seen multiple times waxing the truck to keep the red shiny. Chick was one reason I had always believed that Permanent Winch Truck Operators were valuable classifications. They took better care of the equipment. If Chick was on the trouble call at night, he would go to get a 301 Copper Squeeze-On from the side bin without a flashlight and bring the connector back to the lineman without any hesitation. He knew every inch of his line truck.

LEARNING THE TRADE

Mike Tucker, the Apprentice, and I were in the stake body truck hauling material to a job off Second Street at Memorial Park. I had never driven a five speed with a split axle transmission before. So, Mike immediately let me "drive" back to Riverside Drive across Macon. I learned very quickly when to shift split axle and when not to. The truck must be under power and load or the axle will not move. It makes a whining-clicking sound as you are coasting along. Mike was laughing his tail off, watching me try to engage the transmission. It embarrassed me to death. There were no schools to learn from back then, other than on-the-job training, better known as the "University of Hard Knocks". Either you got it or did not. If you did not, you had to go somewhere else.

A crew that consisted of seven men was called a "Bull Gang." The "Bull Gang" was a hard-working, tough group of guys. We did not always have enough vehicles to ride in, so some of us rode in the back of the line truck, fondly called the "Mother-in-Law". We holed up under a sliding cover over the bed of the line truck. It was not bad back there in summer, but winter was not pretty. Warmer days were spent standing up and hanging on back corners, watching the traffic go by. We saw many interesting sights from the back of those trucks. It also gave us a chance to wave at the girls passing us! I will not add details about this because of a comment a friend of mine down in Florida, Ben Browne, made. Ben knows! There are many names and incidents I must not put to print, although the individuals and their families know. The sad fact is that many of those guys are gone now, but not forgotten for sure. The one thing I am most thankful for is that in all the years I worked at Riverside Drive and Key Street, before I left for Jonesboro in 1985, we never had a fatality on any crew I was on. Jimmy Meeks was killed in Milledgeville on Transmission Crew, and Jackie Donaldson was killed in Mt. Vernon on Distribution. Macon Division had a serviceman get killed in Zebulon in a vehicle accident. There were other incidents further out of my world, in other parts of the state, but not at home. I was so thankful for that.

I was an Apprentice working with a "Bull Gang" Line crew in downtown Macon, GA, preparing for a 4kV to 12kV conversion. A portable transformer bank that had been retrofitted, and three 167 KVAs were on a flatbed trailer that could be connected in parallel to a bank on a pole that needed to be upgraded with new dual voltage transformers. We pulled the bank trailer near the bank pole and started connections. The overhead transformers had been modified with UD bushings on the Hi Side of the transformers, so we could use UD Cable as primary connections to the system. There was a 4/0 Quadraplex service that would be phased, and rotation verified, so we could parallel with the service of the overhead bank. This allowed the crew to both maintain service to customers without outage and to de-energize the OH transformers and switch old straight 4kV transformers to dual voltage transformers. A load check and amp readings were taken to ensure that the single 4/0 Quad service could be maintained. Everything looked good at 9:00 AM. The temporary bank was energized and phased correctly. The voltage check on the 4/0 Quad and rotation were verified. All connections were made on secondary, and the overhead bank was de-energized. There was no interruption of service as the overhead bank was rebuilt with new transformers, equipment arms, switches, and arresters. My job that day was to guard the flatbed trailer and take amp readings on the 4/0, to be sure the load was not increasing on services to exceed the 4/0 Quad. All went well for the first few hours. The overhead bank was feeding a soft drink bottling company. When the load was put on the 4/0 Quad Service, I checked the amp reading at around 150 Amps on each leg of Quad. We did not know that the bottling plant went into full operation later in the day. I rechecked the load later and found almost 400 amps on each leg. I touched the insulation on each hot leg. It was so hot that the insulation was about to melt. Panic mode set in and we quickly restored the overhead bank, since the new transformers had been installed and connected back up. We were able to get the OH bank back in service before an unscheduled outage occurred. As a result, another 4/0 Quad was placed parallel to the one on the portable bank. We had no problems after that. Because of a lack of proper planning, that job taught us a lesson. Always check the history on maximum load. A demand meter can tell you what you need to know. Rule of Thumb: if the maximum KWH demand is greater than the KVA of the transformers or maximum load on the secondary conductor, change the plan.

THINGS I SAW

In the winter months, when the Capital work would fall off, the crew would receive orders to go out to rural lines and walk them. We inspected all poles and arms, checking for rotten poles or damaged cross arms. I rode in the back of a bucket truck to Gray, Georgia one cold, misty, rainy day in a rain suit. There were four of us and I, being the "Grunt", had no place to sit up front. We walked the circuit out, hammering poles from the substation in Gray to the end of each circuit. James, Georgia was ten miles to the southeast, Roundoak was due east toward Milledgeville, and Way Side was fifteen miles to the north. I spent many winter days riding and walking the lines. I found interesting cases of poles and equipment that had trouble calls reported, cut in clear, to be repaired later. I found a single-phase tap with the jumper removed, de-energized, with the pole laying on the ground. Someone had taken a chainsaw to cut the pole down to steal the transformer coil. Transformer coils were copper back then.

I was still on Jay Walker's Line Crew in June when I experienced my first hurricane in August of 67'. Jay's crew did not go on the storm that time, and I was so disappointed. I had heard so many stories about trips made to Florida and down on the Georgia coast by others and thought that would be exciting. We stayed home to keep the lights on in Macon. Ironically, the storm team went to Florida, where the storm was predicted to make landfall, and as storms sometimes do, it turned and made a straight shot to Macon, Georgia. Everyone had gone to Florida, so we had a skeleton crew to catch local trouble. Then, along came the residual of the hurricane, which put much of Macon in the

Dark. After a long trip back home, the others came rolling in like the calvary, to help us hometown boys out. We had been working around the clock since they had left.

Tree trimming was and still is an issue with trouble and storms in the south. The pine trees were worthless, other than being used for "hot shade and a trouble call", according to John Lane. He was correct. Around that time when tree trimming was realized important, the company wanted all circuits on a 4–5-year cycle for trimming. Trees grow a lot in 4 years with warm weather and a decent amount of rain. I caught my share of trouble calls later in my career. I ended up being a Contractor Coordinator, over six cutting/trimming crews and three bush hog crews, after I made Supervisor.

The first wire pulling job by Jay's crew was at Millirons Substation, off Millirons Road. We had to pull in a new circuit of 636 MCM conductors out of Substation and up what is now Key Street to Millirons Road. Millirons Road was a dirt road that stopped at the creek, west of the Substation. The road would later be completed, with a bridge that would meet on the west side of the creek and intersect Bloomfield Road. That happened much later, in the '70s. The Macon Mall would be built on that corner: a huge direct buried and cable in conduit UD job, in which we all had a hand. Also, the new Key Street Operating would be built near the Substation. We would move out of the Riverside Drive location to Key Street Operating headquarters in 73'.

That circuit at Millirons brought back two memories that are hard to forget. One, the 636 MCM Conductor had a steel core. When splicing the conductor, a two-piece sleeve had to be installed. The larger aluminum sleeve had to be installed on the conductor and slid back a short distance, to strip away about 5-6" of aluminum on each end, to allow the steel core to be spliced. Once the steel core had been crimped by a hydraulic crimping machine (hand pumped in those days), the aluminum sleeve could then be slid back in place and centered over the steel sleeve for compression and completion of the splice. I had been asked to prepare the conductor for splicing. I removed

Legends of an Ole' Lineman

the aluminum strands on both ends and was about to install the steel sleeve for splicing. About that time, a car full of visitors drove up. Carl Funderburke, District Engineer, and Lee Saunders, the safety guy, got out and proceeded to watch the splicing. The lineman immediately took over and slid the aluminum sleeve over on the conductor, put the ends together, and started the crimping. I was standing there with the steel sleeve in my hand, and no one answered when I asked, "What do I do with this?". I had to get ratchet bolt cutters out, cut the sleeve out and start all over. I never forgot to put steel sleeves on again. There were plenty of red faces that day, with all the "bosses" watching…Oh Boy!

I was given a "Zip Stick" extension stick to open a switch and remove the fuse barrel on a job one day. It was an old Kearney switch that was easy to get out of the barrel hanger, once you knew how. The first time, you will significantly lose control of the stick and drop the fuse barrel, or have it slide down the hot stick and hit you, if you do not get out of the way. I learned a lesson that day. Jay embarrassed me that day in front of the entire crew. You had to have thick skin in those days. No Helper was cut any slack. If things like that bothered you, you might need to be a Meter Reader or in another position, not requiring the energized work.

Line Crews were a hard bunch to work with, but once you were there, you would not want to be anywhere else. We were a tight-knit, extended family of like-minded individuals, who were not afraid of hard work and hazardous challenges. I was fortunate to be a part of that team. Some of the best days of my career were spent as a Lineman on those crews. I cherish the relationships and the memories that were made. The storms that we worked on and customers that we were able to restore the power to. A very satisfying job to say the least.

My first ice storm was in Atlanta, in January of 68'. Gene "Fat Dog" Moore and I drove a line truck up to Atlanta. It was a short storm; we were only there for about 4-5 days. I went on many more storms during my years as a Helper, Truck Driver, Apprentice, and Lineman. Some were very memorable, and some I wanted to forget. I remember Gene

Conger and I went on one storm with Duke Power, during a hurricane. We almost left a Hi-Ranger stuck on the right of way and flooded up to the doors because we did not want to climb the pole. Gene knew he could get close enough to reach it, about 14 paces off the right rear corner. That model went about 10 degrees over the top, dead center. He got about 18 steps away, bogged it to the frame, and then the right of way was filled with water. Not a good day. It two a Tree Crew's Bucket truck and another truck winch to pull it out. That was after we had dug out the mud in front of the tires to put "skid boards" for the truck to roll on. Gene was not the most popular person after we had worked half a day to get his truck out of the bog hole.

TOUGH DAYS

The first accident fatality I responded to as a GPC employee involved a police car in pursuit of a vehicle on Vineville Avenue. They were both traveling over 100 mph, when the police car lost control and hit a pole in front of the Krystal Restaurant. The police car was torn in half, sending the front half of the car into the Shrimp Boat Restaurant, across the street. When Gene Conger and I got there, the trouble man on shift was Gene "Cut it in the Clear" Copeland. He immediately sent us to pick up a line truck to hold the pole, since half of the police vehicle was wrapped around it, causing the wrecker to not be able to pull the car apart to rescue/retrieve the deceased officer in the vehicle. He was in the passenger side of the police car. The cruiser was torn in half. The vehicle's motor traveled another 100 feet and struck a building just beyond the curve. The vehicle struck the pole on the passenger side and the impact crushed him. Not a pretty sight, but one that I would get accustomed to, since I answered every trouble call from that time on. Friday and Saturday nights were the most active. There were many DUI's back then, which, unfortunately, provided many OT hours for us at GPC.

The trouble men that worked the 24-hour rotating shifts were mostly senior employees. They took the trouble man jobs because they didn't care to work on the "Bull Gangs" anymore and didn't mind the shift work. Dolfie Thomas, Ronnie Crutchfield, Hugh Wright, Ralph Cameron, and Boney Currie were just a few of the Trouble men. Corporate office payroll would have to call Boney Currie to get him to cash his payroll checks before they expired. He was a fun guy to work with. I heard Ralph Cameron on the radio one night when we were working a severe thunderstorm state that, "The Bolt of lightning was a wide as the hood of the Trouble Truck". I dearly loved all those guys. Gene Copeland had worked the midnight shift as a Troubleman for over fifteen years. He told us that he stopped counting the fatalities that he had responded to at twenty. As the city grew, roads expanded, causing poles to sit on the curb line, drivers of vehicles making the slightest mistake deadly. Later, I was a Lineman on a crew that changed out a broken pole off of Cornfield Rd. with three fatalities in one vehicle; it was a terrible sight. And once again, we had to get a line truck on the pole for them to pull the car off of it, without dropping all the primaries to the ground. This happened a lot back in the 70s.

LEARNING CONTINUES

The first Substation I ever walked into was Vineville Substation off Pio Nono Avenue at Roff Avenue. I was fascinated when I entered the Substation. I was told, "Put your hands in your pockets and don't take them out until you are outside of the gate". We were there to get an "R" Switch (one shot) on a breaker in the Substation that Jay Walker's crew was working on. A substation tech was working in the station, testing some other breakers; Harris Floyd was his name. I asked Mr. Floyd, "do you ever get tired of hearing the hum of the Substation Transformer?". He smiled and said, "if it ever quit humming, we would have problems". He said, "it would be quieter than a rat peeing on a cotton ball". I almost choked from laughing so hard. Harris would later be promoted to Substation Supervisor. Super smart man when dealing with anything in a Substation.

All training in those days was done "on the job", or by trial and error by the crews. We never had a class on new equipment. I was taught how to operate an R 40 Ditch Witch, and then an Olm Steele Ditch Witch, working on an expansion of Wells Mobile Home Park. The belief about the "new" Under Ground Distribution system conductor was, "just dig a ditch and put it in the ground; don't worry, it will last 100 years". That is what they said about that first #1, #2, and later 1/0 AXN Direct Buried Cross Link External Concentric Neutral cable. We were back reconductoring in less than eight years of some of the first cables we put in the ground. The Copper Concentric was being chemically corroded and oxidized by ground chemicals. This was a hazard because now, return neutral current was on all other utilities attached to or near the electric utility system. Cable, telephone, gas, and water pipes: all conductive. This increased risk to other utility employees and had to be corrected.

The UD System had the unexpected outcome of the oxidation of the external concentric neutrals. The neutrals of 1/0 and 4/0 Services would disappear. The UD system then was a Single Conductor Earthen Ground return system for primaries. This would burn up all the 120-volt appliances in a home. I pulled a bunch of # 6 Copper Tie wires to the next-door neighbor, to get a neutral on trouble calls, until we could replace the service. GPC did not adopt a "cable in conduit" philosophy, which remains true today. In 1978, the company started installing all UD cables with insulated, weatherproof Primary Cable Neutral, replacing everything that was External Neutral in the ground. It took years. Some areas were much worse than others, so cable lasted a bit longer in those areas. After attending workshops and conferences later in my career, I discovered that was happening everywhere. We live and learn.

DRAFTED IN ARMY

In 1968, just as I finished my time as a Helper, my career at Georgia Power was interrupted. I was selected to be drafted into the U.S. ARMY that May, right in the middle of the Vietnam War. I did not have a deferment, so I was a part of the most significant largest draft of 19-year-olds in the history of the Selective Service System. 43,000 were drafted that month in May of 1968. I was off to Ft. Benning, Georgia for Basic Training. Spent 8 weeks at D421, Sand Hill Basic Training Company at Ft. Benning, and then up to Ft. Monmouth New Jersey in Signal Corps for my AIT in Microwave Communications. Vietnam was raging and the US in the middle of the nastiest war since the Korean Conflict. I had been drafted in as a "Ground Pounder", headed for Ft. Polk, Louisiana after Basic Training. I signed up as a Microwave Relay Station Operator to avoid the rice paddies and nasty stories we had heard about. I passed the electronics test and was then assigned to Ft. Monmouth, NJ, for AIT. I never made it "in the country" because of an accident in AIT that put me at "4A" on Selective Service System. I was discharged with a 10 % Disable Veteran benefit. I recovered from the neck injury at Ft. Monmouth's Post Field House.

I was reclassified by the Selective Service System as "4A" and found myself back in Georgia. I was allowed to return to the position I had left, working for the world's best company as a Winch Truck Operator, about to make Apprentice Lineman. The FBI called me and offered me a job in Washington DC in the Fingerprint Department shortly after I was booted out of the Army. I very politely declined that offer. I was home and that is where I wanted to be. I did not care to go back north again; it was too cold up there. The FBI job offer was a standard offer to disable servicemen after the Vietnam War in 1968-69. Wonder where I might be now if I had gone that route? Doesn't matter, I am a happy man!

BACK HOME

After I was back home in Macon, I immediately went back to a WTO job. I "rolled" John Fountain off the three-man crew he bid on in my absence. Johnny "Dad" Brassalle and Earnest "Lock Eye"Mooney were the linemen, and I was WTO. That was a great and fun time in my life. We did Overhead and UD work. One day, we had picked up a 40' Class 4 pole from the old pole pile at Central City Park and headed straight down 7th Street to a job near Macon Hospital. All three of us were in the front seat of the line truck. I had no escort on the pole. Turning onto Pine Street, I saw a car attempting to swing out to the middle of the road and pass the line truck as I turned right. I was super careful since I was a new WTO. I felt a slight bump, so I stopped. The top of the pole was out of sight, so I was afraid that the top of the pole had entered the lane during the turn and hit something.

After I stopped, Johnny got out of the truck and immediately told me to turn the steering wheel hard to the left and pull forward slightly. I knew something was wrong. The lady that had attempted to pass me misjudged how far the pole was swinging out and hit the pole. The top of the pole entered the right side of the windshield and exited out of the left rear back corner of the back window. Another lady was also sitting in the front passenger seat; she ducked as the pole passed over her head. It scared me to death; I had never seen anything like that. No one was hurt, thank goodness. Not long after this, we were ensured that another GPC vehicle would follow the line truck transporting the pole and protect the end of the pole from being hit again. This incident was repeated some years later. Bo Parks, Larry Peterson, and I were in

Byron, Georgia and had pulled a 35'5 and two 30'5 poles that needed to be brought back to Headquarters. Larry was driving and Bo was in the middle as we were headed north, out of Byron, on I-75 for Macon. It was a beautiful, hot summer day and not raining. Suddenly, the line truck was out of control and about to turn over. We did not know what was going on until I leaned forward and looked at the mirror on the right side of the truck. I saw a car hanging on the end of the poles. The poles had passed through the car and out the back window. Larry did a great job of keeping the line truck from turning over. We stopped, about halfway jackknifed, in the two lanes of the Interstate. I opened the door, stepped out, and looked back. There was an AMC Gremlin with all three poles sticking completely through the vehicle. I thought of the worst-case scenario: that someone was dead by decapitation. I told Bo that I would call the 911 call into dispatch for a sheriff and an ambulance. Bo ran back to the car and called me to hurry back there. The driver was alone in the vehicle and was alive but unconscious. The driver was passed out, drunk as a hoot! He immediately went into shock, so we had to drag him to the side of the road, put his head downhill, and cover him with an emergency blanket. His lips and fingernails had turned purple and blue, typical symptoms of shock. The Interstate was shut down, and luckily for him, a nurse was stuck in the traffic on her way to work. She had a stethoscope and ran up to check his vital signs. He began to regain consciousness about the time the sheriff and ambulance arrived. He looked up at me, and his only words were, "I hit those poles, didn't I?". "Yes, you did", I responded. Witnesses said he was driving at least 100 MPH before he hit the poles, passing everybody on the Interstate. The floorboard of the car had 6-8 empty beer cans. The car hit the pole trailer so hard, it broke the tie-down winch on the rear of the material trailer. The flag stand and three flags were in the back seat of the car. He had creosote on his white golf shirt, where the poles passed by him. He was one lucky guy and I'm glad no one else was riding with him. Once the nurse checked him out, the only thing wrong with him was that he had emptied his bladder and was soaking wet. The sheriff put the bracelets on him and put him in a police car for a ride to the courthouse. Yep, we made the news that night.

The Labor Crew

Eventually, I made WTO on the "Labor Crew" with Sam "Stringbean" Thompson and the three Laborers, Strobie, Sleepy, and Elmo. Of course, most of our time was spent setting poles or cutting a new right of way for a pull-off. That is when I learned to use a chain saw and sharpen a chain. The crew had an old Farm Boss bow saw for the big stuff: the most dangerous saw I ever used. We had 16-20" bar saws for all other cutting.

The labor crew would stay in front of the floating crew setting poles to speed up the jobs. We set poles in energized 12kV with a line truck and pole shields, no rubber goods. I got to be good friends with the laborers, and we worked well together. Those guys taught me how to cut a tree down safely, long before we had a logging regulation put in OSHA Standards. The labor crew clear-cut a lot of right of way for short single-phase and three-phase pull-offs. Later, vegetation management crews came along. If it were a three or pole takeoff, the engineer would either meet us or drive flagged stakes, usually about 40 feet wide, and we would start cutting the trees. The guys would drop the trees and cut them to pulpwood length for pine. If it were hardwood, it would be firewood length, about 30". I would stack it on the right of way, to be picked up later. Once the trees were down and right of way was cut, the labor crew would come back, set poles, and install the down guy rods. Then, a line crew would go in and pull wire and hang transformers behind us.

We were in Jackson, Georgia, right outside the Substation, setting poles for an upcoming re-conductoring job by Johnny Dupree's

Floating Crew. A pole got away from the guys on the ground, got into a 7.2 kV phase, and started burning. We did not have a bucket; all that was on the pole were fiber shields. Everyone knew the pole was burning in the primary and on fire. Strobie started hollering, "Driver, stay on the truck!". The guys were holding the pole with rubber gloves and wearing overshoes. This was one of the many times I witnessed a pole burning on a primary. It was a Creosote-treated pole, which we were told was 90% conductor. It is a wonder that somebody did not get killed that day. More proof that PPE works.

The Labor Crew was a unique opportunity for many tasks. One time, Stringbean came and instructed the crew and me to load up. We were heading to Jonesboro to pick up an old military trailer they had up there. We had to hook up to it and head to Milledgeville to a State Senator's Chicken Farm. Once we arrived, we all jumped into the broiler house, and loaded an entire trailer load of chicken manure. We went back to Macon and spread it in a certain Company Executive's yard to fertilize his grass. While we were there, I climbed a 40' pole in his backyard to adjust his outside TV Antenna. It wasn't always just about keeping the lights on back then.

I have several memories of that crew. Strobie Johnson was Red Roberts's personal driver, when Mr. Roberts would go south to Brunswick and Kingsland. Sometimes on a job, a pick-up would pull up and take Strobie away to drive Mr. Roberts around. Everybody thought the world of Strobie. I also remember the day that Stringbean had a heart attack and died in the hole on Riverside Drive. I was still the WTO on the Labor Crew. It was a rainy day; all the crews were in the storeroom cleaning and restocking, (busy work), and I had volunteered to go out on a trouble call with a three-man crew. We heard the radio call that someone was down at the hole, and an ambulance was on the way. We found out when we returned that Stringbean was sitting on a wire reel talking and just fell over. It was a sad day. He had worked there a long time and many employees had come up with him on the Labor Crew.

Hurricanes and Storms

The first hurricane I can remember was Camille in August of 69'. I had just returned from my stint in the US Army and was on Johnny Brazelle's three-man crew, with Earnest Mooney. Everyone was excited about going to Biloxi, MS. But, because I was on a three-man crew, I did not go on that one. The makeup of storm teams with all the logistics had not been considered and developed. Back then, there was no "balancing the OT" with the amount each worked, so the large crews went first. If there were any follow-ups after the first two weeks, the first crews out would come home, and the company would backfill as needed. Camille was a history-making storm and one of the most powerful to strike the Coast at that time. Crews worked down there on Southern Company System for weeks. I later worked many Storms, Tornadoes and Ice Storms as all Linemen do. That was the time that was most enjoyable to see lights come back on and hear the customers thanks.

"Dad and Lock Eye"

I was working with Johnny and Earnest one day in Gray, Georgia, changing out a Single-Phase primary, 40' Class 4 pole. Johnny ordered me to get in the bucket of an old Holland, with three-handle straight hydraulic controls. He wanted me in the bucket to help tie in the #2 ACSR conductor on an I-9 insulator. When I asked him if he was sure about it, he explained that he would climb the pole and be up there with me. This was before I performed ties, and I had a #2 armor rod and #4 soft drawn aluminum tie wire. Johnny had installed guts on the phase for me to dig the hole and set the pole. Once we had the pole plumbed and tamped, he said, "OK Driver! Get in the bucket. I will be up there in a minute". This is the first time I can remember doing energized work. I had less than three years with GPC and a year of that was spent in the Army. I was not scheduled to go to Apprentice School for several more months. So, everything I was shown was all I knew, with no "formal" training yet. I took a split blanket with me and went up to the new pole top pin we had installed on the ground, before the pole was set. All poles came with pre-bored 4" and 8" holes for the pole top pin. I installed the split blanket and waited for Johnny to get close before I uncovered the primary conductor. The next thing I knew, Johnny was standing across from me, asking me what I was waiting for. I uncovered the primary by sliding the hoses back just enough to install the armor rod and set the conductor in the saddle of the I-9 insulator. He stepped up the pole and put his hands on the 7.2 kV primary, and I could not believe he did that. I asked Johnny, "Is this a safe thing to do?". He said it was okay and told me not to worry. I had been trained enough to know that we did not work hot primary voltages when standing on a pole. That was to be done only from a bucket truck. Linemen at GPC have never worn sleeves, only 18" cuffed Class II rubber gloves. He showed me how to install the armor rod and make a straight-line aluminum tie, and I never forgot how to after that day.

In those early days, the lineman would get the Helpers and WTOs in a bucket and show them how to install rubber covers, line Hoses, and guts (or eels, as they were called) on conductors. My first encounter with energized primary was on a 4 kV. Touching energized 4 kV was not much different from the feeling of secondary conductors. When touching a 7.2 kV Primary, I found the vibration and buzzing was different, with a slight arc to anything metallic. Cutting pliers, bolt cutters, and squeeze-on tools produced that "feeling" of power that this was something much stronger than I was. That was exciting for a 19-year-old. The senior linemen wanted to see the reaction of the "newbie" when they put rubber gloves on, touched the energized primary, and felt the vibration of the 7200 volts in their hands.

Some new employees did not like that and immediately decided to go to another department. I loved that feeling, and later when the company upgraded many parts of the system to 25 kV, it was an even stronger feeling! I never got tired of the exhilaration of having control of something that could kill you with one error in procedure. I enjoyed the feeling, until I touched 500kV line barehanded and became a member of the "Society of Energized", as it was called. Back in the 70s, when GPC first upgraded our Transmission system to 500 kV, it was a practice to have employees that wanted to suit up in the gray metallic suits and boots to go up in buckets and have that experience of contacting energized conductors. Jerry Broome, Big Jim Handley, and I had visitors at the Klondike Training Center from Hawaii Electric. We set up a condor, suited up, and let the folks from Hawaii go and touch the 500 kV bundle conductors at a dead-end tower in the Klondike 500/230 Substation. Jim went up, got out of the Class "A" Condor bucket, and was sitting on the three-bundle conductor dead-end when

Jerry had a group of the Hawaii Electric employees with him and went up. They "wanded on" to the bundle off the toe of Jim's boot. I thought those guys from Hawaii would have a heart attack. It was a new adventure for them, for sure. I see barehand employees today on social media taking the bonding cable off the bundle and contacting energized 500, 345, and 230 kV, energizing themselves and the bucket through their hands. They need to consider what might happen if the boom was to break down at the moment, they were in contact with no bonding cable. The result would not be good. They would instantly become a memory to their families and friends.

Apprentice Lineman

T he" Apprentice School" I attended was a two-week event, held off Main Street in Macon before the East Macon Housing Projects were built. It was mid 69', after I returned from the Army when I was instructed to report to the Apprentice Training Field, which was nothing but an open field with several poles set. It was simply a climbing school. The company wanted proof that newly promoted Apprentices could climb and handle themselves on a pole. The school was led by two existing line crew foremen with extensive experience, and who did not mind climbing poles. There were no dedicated trainers back then. Everything we learned was "On The Job Training". The Apprentice School was learning and a physical abilities test. We mostly just climbed poles and framed off the pole until the instructors were satisfied, we could be considered Apprentices as jobs were opening up. The company really did not want to award an Apprentice position that hadn't been "proof tested" in a school.

One of the tasks was to take an 8' 5' X 5" cross arm with a pole gain on it, a P-6 pin, and I-9 Insulator on just one end (unbalanced load) and pass it back and forth as two apprentices climbed in tandem together up a 40' pole. That was a challenging task for even a young man. It did wash one or two out of the class. There were 12 in my class. One Apprentice went to the Porta-John for a "break" and fell asleep with all his tools still on sitting on the stool. He left the class to read meters.

When I first made Apprentice, the Cut-In/Cut-Out Service truck was one of the first stops in the "development" for a new Apprentice. Learning to catch trouble and climbing poles and installing cut-ins were

42

the basic tasks. I remember the first Fire Call I had: I was on the West Side Cut In truck and we were given a fire call at Forsyth Street and Monroe Avenue. It was an older house that had a breezeway through the middle of the structure. The kitchen was to the left of the breezeway and the living quarters were to the right. When Albert Smith and I pulled up, the house was burning on the kitchen side. The house meter was in the center of the breezeway, about halfway through the opening toward the back of the house. Company policy was to pull and retain the meter at any cost. The fire was burning hot on the kitchen side of the breezeway, so a fireman came up, gave me Turn Out Gear, and went into the breezeway. The Fireman was carrying a 2' line to clear a path to get to the meter. We ran into the breezeway, I pulled the meter, and we quickly ran out. What an experience that was. I smelled like smoke all day after that. I later found out that Riley Bennett, a buddy of mine from high school, went to work at Macon-Bibb County Fire Department about the same time I went to work at GPC. I told him he could have that job. The company later decided that Apprentices and Linemen had no business running into burning houses to pull a meter. Thank goodness, I didn't have to do that anymore.

The Apprentice Lineman years were exciting. All Apprentices were required to spend time on the Cut-In/Cut-Out Service Trucks. The idea was to get as much experience as possible, preparing the apprentices to take care of themselves as the Lineman job was not too far in the future. I started as Apprentice on the East Macon Cut-In truck, with Bennie Britt. That was an experience. The Cut-In trucks ran new OH services for houses or set UD Temporary Service Poles. They also caught squirrel calls or any other trouble that could be handled by a service truck with no bucket. We had a 1-ton open bed truck with a reel of # 2 Triplex, used to run the services. There were many days when Bennie and I would be in Gray, Georgia at 3:30 PM, with two reconnects between us and headquarters, only to get a lights-out call. Bennie would stop for a "coffee break" on the way to the lights-out call. I would get so aggravated, wanting to get off on time. It did not matter;

we stopped at Cleo's Restaurant, "come Hell or high water". There was a young server that Bennie liked to talk with every day. There was one event where I gained much respect for Bennie's knowledge. He did teach me a lot.

We had started a routine day with a rewire and had to replace a three-wire #6 copper service with #2 triplex. I put on my hooks and belt to climb the pole, tied a running line on the triplex, and took an Extendo to open the cut out on the transformer pole. I cut down the old number 6 copper. Bennie got the extension ladder to the house and waited until I had the transformer out to cut the old service off the house knobs. The new service had a 2" mast pipe through the soffit and Bennie strapped a mast bracket on it and hung the service off. He hollered, "go ahead and sag service". I had climbed to the working position at the secondary bus. This pole had an open route secondary on three spools, called I-20, 12" apart on the pole. The neutral was in the middle at this location. I cut the old service down and immediately pulled the triplex up the pole to sag it. It was a short service, so I unwrapped hot legs to give me enough # 4 to slide through the I-20 spool and pull the service through without using jack straps. The service was only about 50' long. As I put the #4 neutral through the spool, the tail of the new service contacted one of the hot legs of the secondary bus. There was a 120-volt arc. I looked up at the switch; I knew that it was open but questioned it. There was no "tracking" evidence, so I called Bennie and told him what had happened. Bennie said, "Come on down and let us look and see what is going on". We walked two spans down to an intersection. There was a junction pole there: the secondary bus from two transformers dead-ended in the same spool. It just so happened that the transformers were on the same phase, and the hot legs phased out, so there was no trouble with phasing when the two transformers were re-energized. The contract crew that had changed the poles out had created an overhead "spot network" between the two transformers, four spans and two streets apart. Now, there should be no questions as to why the OSHA Regulations are worded the way they are for the protection of the employees. We did not have OSHA Regulations then, and it was expected that everyone would do the right thing. No one makes these mistakes intentionally, but mistakes can and do happen because we are all human. That little event could have been deadly but was not. I learned the valuable lesson of not making assumptions. Opening a switch does not mean that the equipment is now de-energized. It just means "the switch is opened". Thank the good Lord for those lessons.

I spent a few months with John Lane on the South Macon Cut-In truck as an Apprentice. John was unique. He taught me a lot about running a case of trouble, particularly on open neutrals on a 240-volt service. We also had to disconnect quite a few services due to nonpayment, when the customer would reconnect the meter by cutting seals and removing boots. I learned a few tricks from John on how to fool customers rather than just cut service down because some of them were savvy about our methods. One of the best ways to cut service: At the hot legs, tape up the ends and then tape them back together to make it look like it was not cut at all or a splice. It worked well on a house on a dirt road. We would toss some dirt and dust back on the jumpers, and they would never see the tape. I loved the old round meter bases, where you could pull the meter and unscrew the tab on the back that made the connection through the meter. The customers never could figure that one out. They would cut the seal and remove the meter. There were no Disconnect Sleeves on meter spades. The customer had no choice but to pay the bill.

There was a time when we had a call to investigate a service that had a history of a high amount of usage each month because suddenly, the bill dropped by more than 50 %. John and I went out to address thinking it was a bad meter. We went to the meter base, cut the seal, and pulled the meter, but the AC Unit kept running. Oops! It was a service with a meter base on one side of the house. They had an entrance cable from the meter base, through the attic, to the location of the meter and panel in the rear of the house. The sneaky rascal knew what he was doing. They got in the attic, opened the SE entrance cable, and tapped two hot legs up to the entrance cable and carried it to the AC disconnect- free electricity for a little while. I found another one on a UD Service that had been dug up and tapped into on the line side of the meter base. One of the best was when the dispatcher gave us a call from a 911 dispatcher about a flash in a meter base. We found two butter knives in the meter base and the victim was in the emergency room.

LINEWORK

I learned so much from many great employees, who opened the door to my future. Like the cold night Chappie Vaughn and I changed an angle pole out on Pio Nono Avenue. The conductor certainly sagged too tight when it was installed, and the pole should have been framed as a vertical angle with clamp-type insulators rather than the flat steel arm with angle clamp insulators. The pole had more than a 25-degree turn flat, which was too much for the pole top pin. We wanted to keep everything hot, because of the businesses up and down the street. We installed the new pole next to the one that had been broken by a vehicle accident. I do not remember who the Foreman was that night, but he wanted to return to the same configuration. We had the pole framed and started transferring the phases. The field side and middle phases were not too difficult, but when we started on the roadside phase, we had to install a clevis on the roadside clamp insulator and use two sets of ¾ ton strap hoists to be able to control the strain. Chappie and I worked together to sag the conductor and get back in position to install the armor rod and lay in the angle clamp insulator. Chappie and I had to pick up at the same time with equal pressure to keep the insulator from breaking off the arm. With each click of the hoists, you could see the insulator move one way or the other, under the strain. If either of us got ahead of the other, we would risk breaking the insulator. We were working the job from the roadside because we couldn't get a bucket on the field side of the pole. The houses were too close to the road. We knew the conductor would come straight to our heads if the insulator broke. It sure did feel good to get the conductor in the clamp and tighten it up. This was an example of skilled labor and a lot of patience.

I spent some time with Albert Smith on the West Side Cut-In Truck. Albert was the neatest guy. He was born in North Carolina. I'm still not sure how he wound up in Macon at GPC, but I was glad he did. He was like a father to all the Apprentices he ever worked with. One of his favorite sayings I never could quite figure it out was, "we have to go over and hope them out". Why he said hope rather than help, I never knew. Albert's philosophy was that when we did not have an order and a permit to set a meter on new construction, we would ride the new subdivisions looking for completed houses. When we found one with a mast pipe up, we would "run a spare". If the mast pipe were up, or the mast and meter base was installed, we would go ahead and run a service to the house. So when the meter order and permit would come in, all we would have to do is set a meter. A tremendous number of new houses were being built back in the '70s. I remember going through a 1000' reel of triplex one morning and had to go to headquarters to get another reel loaded after lunch. I did so much climbing in those days.

In the wintertime, Macon never really got much snow. However, ice storms were almost routine in January, February, and March. Albert and I would head toward the north side of Macon on Forest Hill Road and Wimbish Road to look for ice to form on the tops of the tallest pine trees when we had northeast wind and misty rain conditions. That was Albert's way of giving everyone notice, regardless of what the weather forecast was calling for. Albert rarely missed calling an ice storm. The same was true in the northeast of the Macon District in Gray, Georgia. It was the first place to always ice up.

There was one night that it was 30 degrees and pouring down rain. Ice storms usually start as a misty drizzle, rather than pouring rain. I was called in as an Apprentice, and blue slipped to Lineman, because no one wanted to work in those conditions. I had another Apprentice and a Truck Driver with me on this night. The call was out on Gray Highway, about 10 miles northeast of Macon, with nothing other than a 35' service pole broken by an automobile. The transformer was across the highway, so there were three 1/0 ACSR conductors secondary bus feeding two services off the broken pole. Around 3 AM, we loaded a pole and headed out. It just got colder, and the rain was heavier by the time we got to the job site. By the time we got a new pole in and lights back on, it was daylight, and the temperature had dropped even more. Everything around us had 1/4" of ice on it. By then, we were getting lights-out calls further north in Gray, Wayside, and Roundoak. We worked for a few more hours before they sent us home to pack our bags and head to Atlanta. It took about ten days to get everything back on there. I hated ice storms. I would have rather worked two hurricanes than one ice storm.

STORM WORK OT

S torm work seemed to come around often in the summer. I remember a terrible storm (not sure if the storm was a tornado or straight-line wind), in late spring/early summer. I was married to my first wife, June. We were just back from our honeymoon. It was a Saturday Morning when the phone rang. The area around Milledgeville and Eatonton, Georgia had been hit hard by severe thunderstorms. So, we went to help the local crew. We worked until late afternoon and were on the way back toward Macon when another storm blew in. Charlie Tidwell was driving the bucket truck, and I was riding "shotgun." It was hot, so we had the windows down to get the "2 and 50" air conditioning: two windows down at 50 MPH. Lightning struck a big pine tree right beside us as we drove down Highway 441. It was so close that we could feel the heat of the lightning strike as we were driving by. That got my attention! Another lightning strike in King Street Station in Jonesboro happened one hot summer afternoon. I have a saying: "lightning can only do one thing: anything it wants to do. Just get out of the way, let the lightning have its way, and then pick up the pieces". I once watched lightning strike three single-phase pole reclosers and blow the tops off all three. Lightning struck the 500 kV line and locked the Air Blast Breaker in Tara Station in Jonesboro, Georgia. It was not supposed to happen. The recording voltmeter indicated 2 million volts, and the frequency meter was also pegged at 200 cycles per second. Who knows what the lightning strike was? I am sure that most linemen have stories of damage by lightning strikes.

Harvey "Bo" Hall almost got killed on another occasion between Gray and Roundoak. We were working there when a storm came up. I immediately got on the front porch of an old, abandoned farmhouse to wait out the rain, while he was getting something off the trailer of line truck. Lightning struck nearby and Harvey was standing on the ground, touching the trailer, at the time of the strike. He hollered like he had been shot. There were old-time sayings about the weather: "8 drops an acre is a legal rain" and "a chicken's head is not much larger than my thumb, and it knows to get out of the weather"—These were some of the things we used to say during storms.

Blue Slipped to Lineman

Being an Apprentice on a Line crew back then was interesting. One day, I may be in a bucket working on a job with another lineman. The next day, I might be on the ground as a "Grunt". It depended on the job and how many linemen were out on vacation or sick. I was an apprentice for a more extended period due to a slow-down in promotions. The early 70s were a tough financial time, and there were "cutbacks" due to the construction of the first Nuclear Power Plant built on Southern Company, Plant Edwin I. Hatch in Baxley, GA. GA. The cost overruns caused a massive cutback in pro-motions, so I spent an extra year as an apprentice, which was OK. I was "blue slipped" to Lineman constantly, so I received bottom Lineman pay, working primaries daily, with all the overtime I wanted. Once the crew was comfortable with a young Apprentice, they would routinely swap out a bucket, and the apprentice and one lineman would be in the air. If it were a junction pole or a reconductoring job, cutting in a set of gang switches, I learned a lot from some of the best linemen in the business. There were positions eliminated that required senior employees to "roll" other junior employees to keep their jobs. Some employees had to leave Macon and go to outside districts in order to maintain their classifications. It was a tough time for all of us. I was the Senior Apprentice on the list and when it was over, there were three men that had been rolled out of lineman clas-sification back to apprentices. I remember newly hired Helpers had to roll all the way to vacancies in power plants to work at GPC. The delay cost me a lot, because your ability to bid on jobs was strictly based on seniority and grade.

I held Helper and Truck Driver time in Macon District until 1972. I successfully bid on and received an Apprentice Lineman on the Dublin, GA Transmission Crew. The jobs moved fast back then, and I never even reported to Dublin before I was able to bid on an Apprentice Lineman position in Macon. Finally, in August 1972, I made Journeyman Lineman at the Jonesboro Operating Headquarters. I stayed on a line crew in Jonesboro until a job became available with a line crew back in Macon later that year

Those early years were an exciting adventure for a young man. I was not afraid of anything then and was willing to tackle a thunderstorm if I could figure out where to grab hold of it. The experience I had gained in the early years made me feel ten feet tall and indestructible. I still did not realize just how hazardous the job was. I was told many things in those early days. One was, "rubber gloves are a lineman's best friend". I realized much later just how accurate that statement was. Another piece of advice was, "It ain't dead until it's grounded". I discovered later that grounded didn't always mean dead. And the word "Dead" is not found in in Safety Regulation anywhere. "It" is not "Dead" when it is grounded. The System is Deenergized and grounds provide a parallel path around the worker. All this was discovered much later in my career. That will be a story in the next book, covering my years as a trainer and consultant, after being a Lineman. I did learn to respect, but not fear working with electricity. As my experience grew, I became more comfortable with line work and set my mind on being the best Lineman possible. I listened to Lee Iacocca at Chrysler back in those days: "Lead, follow, or get out of the way". I was like most all other linemen; I did not like to be told what to do or how to do a job. Just give me the job and leave me alone to work it. As a Helper and a Truck Driver, I was given many opportunities to be blue slipped to the bottom pay grade to the next highest classification when other employees were on vacation or a trouble call came in late at night. Or sometimes, when no other WTOs, Apprentices, or linemen were willing to come in. I never turned down any opportunity to learn more and make OT.

Bucket Trucks and Linemen

I spent most of my time as Apprentice climbing poles. First up and last down was the rule. It didn't matter if you didn't do anything but watch and listen to the linemen in the buckets. As soon as the primaries were secured and covered, Apprentices had to climb and watch. We had many types of bucket trucks at any given time. When I first made Lineman. I had an old Holland Bucket in 72'. It had a round, green, fiberglass upper boom, with a small one-person bucket. I called it an "Ice Cream Cone" because if you ever dropped anything in the bottom of the bucket, you would have to get out of the bucket and go headfirst down to retrieve whatever had been dropped. We finally started getting "Hi-Ranger" buckets before Terex bought out Hi-Ranger. We all thought they were the best bucket ever. I loved the single-man Hi-Ranger bucket: it was 55' and could do so much with it. We had a saying back then that a good lineman and one Hi-Ranger could work two helpers in the ground. There was no material handling boom and winch, so rigging for hot work was a "crown jewel" in my education as a Journeyman Lineman in those days.

I considered myself a lucky man to have had guidance and shared experiences with many of the best linemen in the business. Even the best in the industry makes mistakes, some worse than others. I have learned the lessons of loss of focus, rather than subjective bad decisions. All are human errors but based on different reasons. I have seen the best in the business forget to take the grounds off a primary pull-off and close the line fuse. I have also witnessed the best linemen and crews forget to take the grounds off an Underground Transformer, close the bayonet fuses, and cross-phase primaries with a mechanical jumper. Those kinds of mistakes and errors were learning experiences for all of us. The bad decisions that resulted in contact and fatalities rarely occurred around me when I was coming along. We heard about them; I remember early in my career, there was a fatality in Milledgeville, Georgia. A lineman named Jimmy Meeks was climbing past an old, abandoned, two-conductor "Hi-Line Telephone", making a transposition on one side of an "H" structure. There were miles of the old communications system that had been cut in the clear but was still in "operating condition". It was insulated and isolated and energized through, what I now understand, as "induced voltage" from the 115 kV line overbuild. The I-6 insulators were on locust pins, and Jimmy brushed a bare arm against a copper tie wire when climbing past, lost his grip, and fell to the ground. The pole was also wrapped in hardware cloth (bird wire), to discourage the woodpeckers from ruining the creosote pole. The crew performed CPR, but he still passed away. I was not there but was on the IBEW Investigating Team that went to Milledgeville from Macon to review the accident report for accuracy. I now understand that the accident resulted from a lack of training, total understanding, and work direction supervision. It was a sad day for all of us. Jimmy was a great guy. This accident was the first of many I would help investigate.

Other linemen at that time were George Moxley, Jimmie McDaniel, Bobby Waller, Ronny Spillers, Bill Hammock, Sidney Boyd, and others I owe my career to that taught me line work. I remember a story about Bill Hammock; I loved that man. The story went that when he was a new lineman in Zebulon. The Foreman gave Bill the nickname "Flowers", because he was a "blooming idiot" and never met the Foreman's expectations. Bill had a saying that he used when he would find a rotten pole that I had never heard before. We were at the intersection of Vineville Avenue and Forest Hill Road, when we found a junction pole that was in bad shape. He called in on the radio and said that the pole was "rotten as patter". I ask him what "patter" was. He explained to me that it meant rotten wood. One time, Bill and I were splicing a UD primary, and it was hot as usual. He removed his hard hat to wipe his forehead off and a handful of hair came out with his sweat rag. We didn't know what was wrong at the time. He later went to the doctor and found out that he had some sort of virus that made all his hair fall out. He was bald for a few months and then all his hair came back. The last time I saw Bill, he was singing in the choir at a church we visited. I sure miss that guy, even today.

Jim Swift was one of the toughest Linemen I ever worked for as a Truck Operator and Apprentice. He could make the Pope lose his Religion. I saw him send a brand-new helper for a "wire stretcher" or a "sky hook" several times. That was just part of learning on a line crew. Once, Jim had a medical problem and was in the middle of remodeling his house out in Dry Branch, off Jeffersonville Road. When all the crew members found out, we all went out there and finished installing the paneling in the den. Cecil Brown was the official person in charge of measuring and cutting the paneling. The rest of us were "gophers"- go for this and go for that.

There was another lineman I worked with, named Herschel Stone. He had a stuttering problem all his life but could sing in the choir like a songbird and never miss a note. He would ride around singing choir songs in the Cut-In trucks with me, and if the radio would go off, and he would answer it and could not finish a sentence, he would say, "Danny, answer the radio". The day we were all helping at Jim's, he was measuring a wall for a short piece of paneling to finish a corner. He called out the measurement to cut a piece of the paneling as "one foot and thirteen-and-one-half inches". I thought the house would fall in, and Cecil Brown went nuts. We had so much fun and made so many memories. I will always miss these guys.

Today's linemen would have had a hard time back then, in the "my way or the highway" days. I saw a line crew Foreman, George Stakle, fire a new Helper at 8:00 one morning, for coming to work with bad creosote burns on his face and arms They were from when he had unloaded poles off the rail car the day before at the old pole pile in Central City Park, next door to G Bernd's. G Bernd's was a cattle hide tanning business, a real smelly place. It smelled like death all the time. Lunch on those days was not pleasant. Unloading poles next door to G Bernd's was one of the lousiest jobs you could draw when we were working on Riverside Drive. The Helper was overly sensitive to the creosote and looked like a fried piece of meat that morning. George told him he was not "cut out for the job" if he would react to the creosote that way. He left and never returned. Times have sure changed. Another time, I witnessed a new Helper be fired for being less than five minutes late getting to the loading dock in the morning. Not sure if he had a history of being late, but when he walked up at about 8:05AM, he was instructed to take his lunch box and go upstairs. He never came back. It did not take too many of those lessons to help me understand that walking a tightrope for the first six months was essential and that the Foreman did not put up with too many excuses. There was no such thing as HR or employee concerns back then. After watching and listening, I knew not to be late. I did push the envelope a few times when a bunch of us would pull an "all-nighter" and drag in at 7:30 AM, wondering if we could make it through the day. Oh, to be young and dumb again.

GETTING THE PROMOTION

I was finally successful in bidding on a Lineman job in Jonesboro in 1972. I lived in Macon then but was not going to move to Jonesboro, as some of the other Macon employees had. At the time, we had friends that lived in McDonough, so I rented a bedroom from them. I would go up early on Monday mornings, spend the night Monday and Tuesday, and go back to Macon on Wednesday night to see the family. I'd leave again Thursday morning and spend Thursday night in McDonough, before going home for the weekend. It was a long three or four months that I worked on "Mac" McClendon's crew in Jonesboro. Some other guys from Macon were already up there. Some lived in a boarding house, while others just rented an apartment or a house. I had decided to take the first Lineman job back in Macon when it became available, and I did. I reported to Jonesboro in August for the first time and was able to come back to Macon in November. My time in Jonesboro has its memories. All I heard from Jean Moore and others was, "This is not Macon; this is Jonesboro" like it was a different company. I began to understand how local culture affects the employees working there. The work, spec book, and trucks were all the same, but boy, did they go about things differently! There was one job, a one-span, three-phase extension to build a bank of transformers. I had completed similar jobs in Macon many times. It was in Stockbridge, Georgia, in a small shopping center. The Foreman, Mac McLendon, wanted to see how well the "new guy" could manage the job. So, he insisted that the crew set a new pole, build the bank, dead-end the new primaries on the new pole, and sag the new conductors on an existing energized, three-pot bank dead-end pole. I had always been taught that it was much safer to cover the existing energized and dead-end the new wire and hold in clear and sag the wire on the new pole. "Not in Jonesboro", is what I was told; "This is how we do it in Jonesboro". So, it took about twice as long to sag the four conductors. Trial by fire is what I called it. All went well: a lot of cover and no fireworks. I passed the test that day.

Another job was to cut a line fuse cut out into an existing single-phase pull-off. About three spans from the three-phase line on the single phase, the single-phase line enters a heavily wooded area and often has problems with limbs falling into the line, blowing the line fuse. There was a large subdivision just before the wooded right of way, so they wanted to move the fuse to the last pole before entering the wooded area. I was alone, with an apprentice and it was just me in the bucket. I jumped out the line switch on the take-off pole and built a solid jumper back. Then, I moved the switch location to the new pole and used a mechanical jumper to cut a set of disc insulators in-line, hung the switch, built the jumpers, and removed the mechanical jumper. The entire process took about an hour and a half. Mac looked over the job and never said a word. He just nodded and gave me the next job. During these days, I decided that I never wanted to be that type of supervisor. My philosophy was to recognize what I want repeated and correct things that did not meet expectations. Mac was a great guy and a friend on the job. I always felt he believed he needed to be the "boss" on the job and wanted everybody to understand that. It was another time with a different generational belief. Mac never changed; I did.

BACK ON TWO MAN CREW

After I finally took a Lineman job on a two-man crew, I worked Underground day in and day out. I answered the phone more than most, so I changed out many broken poles on nights, mostly on weekends. One Friday night, I had just finished dinner. By 7:30PM, the phone rang, and we had a broken pole. Before we had the first one changed out, there was another. Before the night was over, we had five total. None were junction poles or banks, so they were not that difficult to change out. That was how we made extra money. Overtime was a way of life for me in the Apprentice Lineman and early Lineman days. I remember one night, a pole was struck by an automobile and broken on Shurling Drive just past New Clinton Road. The gang switch pole was about ten spans out of Hurling Substation. I remember this one because the Macon District Superintendent at the time had stated, "There is no reason that crews can't keep everything hot while replacing a pole or catching a case of trouble". There were many outages and customers were complaining. Amazing how those kinds of statements can bite you in the butt. The pole was broken just below the neutral, above the Communications cable. The primary conductors were 397 MCM. Because of the strain on the angle pole, the top of the pole sheared off and was in the middle of the westbound lane of Shurling Drive. The station beaker operated once and came back hot. So, there was a pole top sitting in the middle of the road, hot. You could stand on the ground and touch all three phases and energized parts. Police blocked off the road, and when we arrived there, we were asked if we could keep it hot and transfer it to the new pole. The new pole would be set on the roadside after the broken stub was removed about 12-15' back from the top of the broken pole. We all laughed and said, "No, drop the breaker". Charlie Tidwell, Gene Conger, and I were there with three buckets and two line trucks. We had a plan to not have too long of an outage. So, we set a new pole, installed the guys, transferred and tied off the TV and telephone cables to the new pole, and pulled the old pole out before we ever dropped the breaker. We installed a new gang switch on the new pole and had six sets of nylon ratchet straps hanging in the dead-end shoes of the new switch before we even tried to move the old pole. Once the breaker was open, two sets of grounds were installed on either side of the broken pole location, the Digger Derrick Truck raised the broken pole top with all the hardware and the conductors to a position almost level with the new pole, and we caught off all six conductors, moving primaries to the new pole. We dead ended the wire, adjusted the closing mechanism, removed the grounds, and made the station breaker back hot. The outage lasted less than an hour. This was not bad but be careful of the statements you make. The mouth can overload other body parts if not careful. No matter how good you are, a pole always needs an outage to work on.

Many other trouble calls involved broken poles. One of the first ones I remember was in Gray, Georgia, near the middle of the downtown area of the city. The crew arrived at the accident scene, and the police had the road blocked off for us. We got there and set up the line trucks. Clinton Station breaker was locked out, so there was a sense of urgency to get the power back on. The circuit was radial back then, and there was no way to switch the circuit out. It was 2:00 AM, and we needed a utility locate (now a One Call). Nope, it was not happening. We obtained clearance by opening a switch and cutting a set of jumpers, grounded on each side of the broken pole, and went to work. We untied all the conductors and floated the ones that had not burned down. I pulled the old stub out and tried to dig out the hole so a new pole could be installed. We heard the gas leak around the third time the auger turned around. The old pole had been installed first, and a gas main had been installed directly under the pole. So, when we attempted to ream the old pole hole out, the teeth on the auger cut the gas line. As you can imagine, this cleared the area; we cut the truck off and ran down the street about 50 yards to escape the gas leak. There was no fire or damage to anything, except the gas main, but we had to wait hours to get the gas cut off and finish changing the pole.

I had several truck drivers come and go. Jerry Kirkwood would wind up as my "Permanent" WTO. He found out he did not want to (or could not) climb a pole, so he washed out of the Apprentice progression. He decided being a Permanent WTO was not a bad job. He later took a Cable Locator position, after I left Macon for a supervisor's position in Jonesboro. However, he decided that it was not for him and returned to a WTO job without losing his seniority. It was a Union negotiated agreement with the company that anyone bidding for a non-covered job could return within 24 months, without losing any seniority. Jerry was an interesting guy. He was a hard worker and was always willing to go the extra mile with very few if any, complaints.

When we were on the two-man crew, we would dig all week, installing cable on weekdays so we could terminate cable and makeup transformers on weekends. We had to take vacation days to have a day off. I remember one small subdivision that Jerry and I installed. It only had 5 Transformers. We wanted to see how many feet of cable and trench we could dig in a day. We loaded up a 2000-foot reel of 1/0 primary cable and drove to the job site, about 20 minutes from the headquarters. Jerry and I had a new R-6510 Ditch Witch and wanted to see what it could do. Everything was located and ready to go, so we started and installed 2300' of conductor and stubbed out all five transformers in one day. I had to go and get a second reel of primary at lunch to get to the UD riser pole on the opposite side of the road. I do not remember the name of the subdivision, but it was where the new Vice president of the Macon Division would live; Gene Barrineau and his sweet wife, Dot. He was one of the best Vice Presidents we ever worked for in Macon. Gene and Dot were bowlers, and Vicki and I were their partners in a four-person mixed league. Bo Parks, Earl Grant, Steve Edwards, Harold Brocklehurst, and many other GPC employees bowled in that league. Dot and Gene remained good friends of Vicki and me after we moved to Jonesboro, back to the Macon area, and then to our current location near Griffin, Georgia. They lived near Stone Mountain, and we would occasionally visit after we stopped bowling with them.

Ken Wall and I were on a trouble call once that required changing out a large, 100 KVA overhead Transformer in a bank. We had been trained to split a transformer for a Wye-Wye bank with an internal connection on three bushing low-side transformers. The helpers and truck drivers got the transformer oil on when disconnecting the four leads to series the coil. Alley Cat - Bad Dog, AC/BD to X1 and X2 bushing. No one ever told us that subtractive to additive transformers coils reversed until much later. I grew up on a 4 kV and then converted to a 12,470 Wye-Wye system. Then, some areas started converting to 25kV, and additive polarity became subtractive H1 and H2, revering the low side bushings. Spec books had to be updated, and we all learned we could take a dual voltage transformer and change it out in a straight additive polarity bank. Ken and I had a 4-bushing low side and we had to series the low sides to replace a three-bushing transformer. We both had thoughts, and then it dawned on us to look at the data plate to verify the bushings. Fun times that look so simple now, but it would have been great to have a class to teach us, rather than be in the field at 10:00PM, trying to figure it out! That is why I love linework and greatly appreciate what goes on in the field. Today's challenges are just as significant. We have learned so much from the past; the industry is training today's linemen much more efficiently and quickly. The "Human Factor" is the greatest challenge in the field today. Some linemen believe they know enough not to follow all the rules to get a job done. When this happens, the wheels fall off the wagon and things go wrong. I spend much of my time training on Human Performance. No one does things intentionally to hurt themselves or a co-worker, but it happens daily. The "why" is what I have been trying to determine. We are all human, and we all make mistakes no matter how good we are or think we are. It does not matter how many times we have performed the same task. Near the end of the next book, I will recount some of the cases I have been asked to be deposed on for opinions and accidents that I have been asked to investigate. You may be shocked as to whom things happen to and how much experience they have.

25 kV Stick School

Harold Brocklehurst and I were "Pole Buddies" during a 25 kV Sticking School at Key Street Operating Headquarters in Macon. I had been on vacation for a week and had purchased a new pair of Red Wing climbing boots. I walked into the headquarters that Monday and was informed that I was assigned to a sticking school for the next three days at the training field. At that time, there was a need to upgrade parts of the system from 12 kV to 25kV, because the load was so high on distribution systems. Breakers in our area were set to trip at 600 Amps, and many were running 500 amps or more during summer and winter peaks. They were selling a lot of air conditioning units and heat pumps. It was too difficult to get approval and build new substations to split the load, so the upgrade was the next best solution. The Union was negotiating with the company to add a "25 kV Linemen" classification and pay a differential for gloving of the higher voltage. I look back on those days and think how that was a challenge since linemen now glove up to 46 kV in locations all over the country. So off to school, we went. There was a training field set up with a three-phase 397 MCM ACSR line with dead ends and angle poles. We could set up almost any situation we needed to use all the sticks, lever lifts, pole crabs, clamps, eye, and holding sticks, etc., to lift and move conductors to change insulators or transfer poles. There was one angle pole that I remember the most. It had an approximate ten-degree angle with the middle phase on a pole top pin. Brock and I climbed up and set up the sticks and lever lift to lift and push the conductor up and away from the insulator so we could simulate changing it out. We had difficulty getting the 397 MCM side tie off the I-9 insulator. The side tie had been used several times and had been bent enough that it was hard to get it started. We had to hold one end with a clamp stick and remove the opposite end of the tie. Once it was off, the "Klondike Trainers" that were there to run the school approved of what we did and told us to go ahead and tie phase back in. We asked for a new side tie but were told, "No, use that one again". I told Brock that it was about to get to be interesting. We attempted to start the side tie back on the conductor, but it was bent so badly now that it was impossible to hold it with a clamp stick to start "rolling" the side tie back on the conductor. We called down to get a new one, and one of the Klondike Trainers said a few ugly words. He stated, "Get out of the way and let me show you how to tie the conductor in correctly". I told him, "Come on up and have at it. I want to watch you!". I knew it could not be installed because it was bent so badly. He came up the pole, grumbling the entire time, saying distribution linemen did not know how to use sticks correctly. I stepped down and around and watched the "show and tell" lesson. I will not identify which trainer it was, but we all knew him, and his reputation preceded him everywhere he went! He took the tie stick, and Brock was holding the free end. Mr. Trainer attempted to install the tie back on the conductor several times and finally hollered, "Give me a new side tie!". Everyone reading this should know what happened next. We had fun with that one.

Bob Rogers was in the same class. Bob had made Apprentice in Macon and was in Apprentice School there, but had worked in Jonesboro for many months before the school. The crews in Jonesboro were the first to convert to 25kV and had been sticking everything because the negotiations with Union on gloving had not been completed and agreed to. They were the best in Division with Sticking Distribution. One of the Klondike instructors bet him he could not stick to a specific task and decided if he did, he would not have to climb the rest of the day, as a reward for completing the task. Bob and his "pole buddy", Jeff Durham, performed flawlessly, completed the tasks, and climbed down. The instructor then told Bob he was not through. This instructor was different from the incident with the side tie, but the viewpoint was identical. Bob called his hand on the bet and won. G.W. Young, Bob's Line Supervisor, was also present at the time of that class, and everyone there had a good laugh.

LINEMAN DAYS

There was a lot of construction and conversions going on in the Macon District. When I started working in the District, I remember that large parts of the territory were operating at 4 kV. The crews converted the area to 12 kV in the early 70's. I remember an apprentice who was working in the Alleys in downtown Macon. There was an Overhead Network in a 25 square block area downtown, in the heart of the city, where all the secondary bus was tied and phased to maintain service to downtown businesses. All secondary buses were connected at every junction pole with # 6 Copper. If one pot in a bank went out for any reason, there would be a voltage drop, making the customers receive low voltage and report dim lights. In that case, we would know that something was in trouble and could look to find it. The bank closest to the dim light call would be the first place we would start looking. The day came when we started opening the jumpers and having service off the banks of transformers near the business. We began converting that system from 4 kV to 12 kV by separating the secondary and rebuilding each bank in the spot network. The Apprentice was in the process of removing the # 6 copper jumpers from the 4/0 Copper dead ends. The secondaries were all on 4 spool racks at terminating points. Not a lot of space between hot legs. If I remember correctly, the Apprentice was Grady Robertson. Grady was removing a 2 Bolt clamp, did not cover up the other energized conductors, and got a 12" crescent wrench between two hot legs, 120/208, at the 4 Spool Rack. When the fire went out, all that was left of the wrench was just the part of the handle in his hand. The end and wrench head were vaporized in the contact and flash. The Overhead network just blinked and never blew a fuse. He climbed down the pole and went straight to bid on a Meterman job in the meter shop, where he eventually retired.

I was a junior on the seniority list when a job came open on Smokie Smarr's Line Crew. I had at least three linemen ahead of me in Jonesboro that could have bid on and got lineman jobs based on seniority, but they did not. Maybe because Smokie was not the easiest Foreman to work for. It did not matter to me; I was home! I was happy to get back to Macon in November, just in time for Thanksgiving! Happy days! I wound up loving Smokie. Once, I went up to a house he was building in Monroe County and helped with the wiring to keep the cost of building down. All employees would pitch in and help build each other's houses. We were not making much money in those days, so it made it more affordable to get the wiring and plumbing installed. A few cases of beer were about all it took. It was a "family" atmosphere back then. We took care of each other. If someone were moving, we would plan it on Saturday Morning to have about 15 pickups show up. We all showed up Tommy Bryan's house one Saturday to force him into a new home he bought in Lake Wildwood. We moved everything in the house in one load each. The guys had everything in his house moved and set in place in the new home in about four hours and were gone. We looked like a caravan coming into the neighborhood. Smokie was replaced by John Lane as Foreman after a short period of time. Ed Lunsford became the new Senior Lineman that I would work with for many months. All we did was reconductor old lines to new and change out junction poles. We were the "go-to crew" for trouble calls/broken poles and demanding jobs.

GROWING THE FAMILY

It was the Fall of 72' and my firstborn, Kim, was on the way. She was born on 2/14/73, our "Valentine Girl." It was good to get back to Macon. I had bought a mobile home and was living in Cross Keys Mobile Home Park, just 5 miles from my office on Riverside Drive. Even though we were about to move to the new Key Street Operating, I was very happy to be close to work. The move would put the office another 6-7 miles away, but I didn't mind. The holidays went well, with no surprises until Key Street Operating Headquarters was completed. We moved the entire GPC from Riverside Dr to Key Street on the west side of Macon. You would not believe how long it takes to move a storeroom, appliance service, transformers, a pole pile and the engineering section. All the crews, plus moving companies, took weeks to get it all moved. We did not think we were ever going to get it all done.

About a month after returning from one of the worst ice storms ever seen in Atlanta, there was a rogue snowstorm in Macon, GA. It was unprecedented and never repeated. Rain changed to snow and fell in wet, heavy flakes as big as a half dollar for 24 hours. When it finally stopped, there was 17" of snow on the ground. Most of the town and the district were in the dark. No one could get around to repair the system without some form of four-wheel drive. This was one of those times when we were unprepared because no one had ever dealt with anything like this. I had a Hi-Ranger bucket truck and getting chains for the single-axle rear wheels was not easy. We all worked many hours a day, for three days, until we started catching up. We also had to call all the troops in. The strange thing about that storm was that just 75 miles to the south or north, there was hardly any snow or trouble. There was a 100-mile-wide path of destruction that no one had seen before. Four days into storm work, I got the call that my firstborn was on her way. I had to stop what I was doing and get a ride to the Riverside Clinic, where Kimberly was born. Record-setting events occurred twice in one week for me. I was now a happy Dad of a beautiful baby and was on top of the world. Piles of snow in the parking lots were as large as tractor-trailer trucks...

I eventually moved the mobile home to Whites Oaks Mobile Home Park, another 5 miles east. That made the commute even further. I lived 18-19 miles from the office, and the commuting costs increased with gasoline increases. We had a fuel shortage back then, much like we have now. Of course, gasoline was not $5.00 per gallon. A lineman's pay was still less than $12.00 per hour. June and I were living there with Kim when we had a 90-mph storm one morning that almost blew the home away. It was then that I sold the mobile home and bought a house on the southwest side of Bloomfield on North Ohara Drive. We were only 4 miles from the office at Key Street, which made for a much easier commute. Kim has since given me two granddaughters, Kaylen and Kristina and Kaylen has given me two great-grandchildren, Easton and Ella! Never thought I would be a great-grandfather!

Ralph Cameron and I were the linemen on a two-person crew sent to Atlanta ice storm in 73'. Mike Garrett was a young Engineer right out of college. Mike went along to be the Team Leader. This might have been his first big storm and this one was a big one. There were over 2000 linemen working in just the Atlanta area. The highlight of the storm was when Mike came to the job site just as we started to work that shift. The storm team had assigned us to be the night crew, working from 4:00 PM till 8:00 AM the following day. It was dark when Mike showed up on the job site. We had about half a street off on a short single-phase pull-off. He stepped out of his pickup truck and was walking through the snow and ice down to my bucket truck. I looked up just in time to see Mike step on and walk down a # 8 Copper primary conductor laying in ice and snow, still hot. 4 kV was not even making a sound in the ice and slush. I hollered at him and told him to get off the wire. He fussed at me saying it didn't matter, since it was dead. I explained that it was energized, and we were about to open a switch to de-energize the pull off. I told him to look at the house with lights on behind him. Mike almost spit his teeth out. About a year before I retired, Mike became the President and CEO of GPC. I reminded him many times after he was promoted that I saved his life that day. He just laughed and often said that he should have fired me for being a smart aleck. Those were the days—the ones I miss. Mike was a great CEO.

In 1975, I was a Linemen at key Street. June and I bought a house in Bloomfield. We had sold the Mobile home and are now living in a nice brick home. We both had great jobs and were "moving on up" in the world. I had figured out that if I had a College Degree I might one day be able to be a Local Manager position or another management-type job. I enrolled in Macon college and set a course on a Business Administration Degree. These were tough days even for a young man. Two nights a week, four hours a night at Macon College, and at least two nights a week of homework. I learned to really appreciate "rainy days" at GPC. They would give me a chance to complete homework and get paid for it! At about the end of the second year, I was burned out. I took Summer Quarters too and never took a break. It was then I was told by an un-named Manager that a two-year associate degree would "do me no good" at GPC and I needed a four-year degree to really make it to a higher level. I really felt frustrated, never finished to bachelor's degree. Most of us felt that Linemen were really not appreciated and were looked down on by management. But we never quit. The only time we felt appreciated was by customers as we restored power during bad storms. I still loved that job and would not change anything. I realized alter everyone didn't feel that was about line crews, just a very few did.

TWIN PINES

Somewhere in the mid to late '70s, management of the Macon Division decided on a special project that all employees could be involved in, if they wanted to. Twin Pines Lodge and Recreation Center was designed and built by GPC employees - such a neat place. I think every employee worked on the building. The substations crews did most of the civil work on the concrete and block. It was a huge log cabin-type structure, with a nice kitchen and outdoor pavilions. The centerpiece was the fireplace that was designed and constructed by the employees. It was a great place, and it was next door to George Aycock's house and land off Heath Rd. George was the "unofficial" caretaker and kept an eye out on the property. George eventually made Supervisor in Brunswick and moved. We started having many safety celebrations and off-site meetings at Twin Pines. I cooked and ate a lot of steaks and Bar-B-Que at that place. The idea to rent out Twin Pines to private parties was thrown around at one point. The property was sold because of a serious incident that occurred there. Even the Bowling Teams would rent out the place for our end-of-the-year banquets and awards ceremonies. All good things must end.

Working Days and Nights

I worked on a big line crew for several years. There were different crew foremen, but there was one that came along that we all thought was one of the best to work for, John Lane. John had been a lineman before I started with the company in 67'. I worked with him as an Apprentice on the southside Cut-In truck, "South Macon Power and Light", as he called it. He was the most likable guy you could ever meet. We hit it off and always worked well together. I started bowling with John in a bowling league and went to local and national tournaments. We had fun. I have never met anyone quite like John. He was one of the most influential mentors during my early years in the industry. He finally made Service Supervisor when Henry Rogers retired. I worked for John again as a trouble man and, for a short while, as a Trouble Dispatcher now called System Operator.

I discovered in 1978 that I had been born with a spinal issue that was not found until I started losing sensation in my legs and feet. I had to have back surgery, a spinal fusion, and was not sure I could come back as a lineman. So, I bid for a Dispatcher's job. I had the surgery the week of Thanksgiving and was back in the Dispatcher's seat on New Year's Day. I bid back to a line crew on an underground Lineman job as soon as the doctor released me the following March. That 1978 bone fusion surgery lasted until August 2019, when that bone fusion had to be removed, and replaced with titanium plates and screws. That story will be explained in the next edition.

ED LUNSFORD

Ed Lunsford and I were the Linemen on John Lanes' crew. We had a series of Apprentices, WTOs and Helpers come and go during the three years that I was on that crew. We were the "Bull Gang". John would request (and get) the most challenging jobs of all. We re-conductored a double circuit of 4/0 copper to one circuit of 750 MCM out of the South Macon sub-Station down off 7th Street. I learned the lesson to never use black plastic tape to hold a jumper in place so I could use a set of ratchet bolt cutters to cut the conductor. We had the two circuits laid out on 5"X5"X11' arms for the dead ends, and a 10-foot wooden arm with spliced-out wooden arms to give us enough room to work the middle. There were no fiberglass layout arms and very few hydraulic tools/cutters back in those days. Ed and I had Chicago pneumatic air wrenches in the buckets, instead of hydraulic wrenches. Laying out the old 4/0 and pulling the new 750 down the middle of the energized double circuit vertical was a job I had never done before. We had the new 750 pulled in, and I taped the conductor to a down guy to hold it in place while I cut the wire. I had cut it a little longer to allow a dea-dend shoe and enough tail to make a jumper. Great plan, but the black plastic tape did not hold the conductor properly under that much strain, or I did not wrap enough tape on the 750. The tape came loose when I cut the wire, and the strain on the conductors brought the tail by me, swinging freely out to the end of the cover I had installed on the ener-gized phase. The 750 was grounded and contacted the energized phase; this caused a flash at the end of the cover and locked out the breaker. It was so embarrassing and also dangerous. Ed was on the other end, and he was the first thing I thought of. Thankfully, it all worked out, and we just made the breaker back hot. I changed my insulate and isolate work practices and started adding additional rubber cover to expand my work zone and protect myself from judgment errors I might make. A Salcor Line Hose (gut) is only 5' long. The extra gut made the protected work area 10' wide.

John's crew would finish one big job and move on to the next one. We finished the Seventh Street job, then started reconductoring a three-phase line at the Forsyth Road substation, near the WMAZ Radio Station Transmitter. We pulled wire a mile at a time, to the end of the three phases on Old Forsyth Road. It took several weeks to complete. We would pull in 5000' of 397 MCM. Further out from the substation, 1/0 ACSR at a time, we transferred the load, tore out old #2 ACSR or #6 copper wire, and moved to the next section. We spent many days out there, which grew my experience even more. I was convinced after a while if linemen couldn't set off old conductors, pull in new conductors, tie in and transfer load without the customer even realizing what we were doing, the linemen need more training and increase skill sets. That is what a Journeyman Lineman should be able to do.

There were many tornadoes, hurricanes, floods, snow, and ice storms over the years. John Lane would say, "We are going to be the heroes and get the lights on!" back on those stormy days. We were all heroes, catching a broken pole or working storm trouble. John was a great friend and one of the best Foreman I ever worked for. He was promoted to Service Supervisor, over the Cut-In and Cut-Out crews and the Trouble men, before he retired. I repeatedly stated to others, "I would climb poles for John Lane before I would work a bucket for another foreman". There was no social media and no recognition of the long hours and hard work that line crews executed on storm work. It is so good to see all the recognition linemen are receiving on social media today for what was done in those days with no recognition at all by the public. The company would award us with a Shirt, a knife, or a hat for getting the lights back on. That was it.

I learned so much and had a great time with this bunch. I learned how to shoot a slingshot with river rocks at the bottles the Helpers would toss in the air during lunchtime. We would cut a stock from wood or fiberglass board and use old rubber gloves for the rubber bands and leather glove covers for the pouch. John Lane was notorious for shooting at Ed and me when we were up in buckets. Regardless of the job we were working on, if John wanted our attention, he would use the slingshot and shoot us with China berries as ammo. If Ed and I were not doing the right thing, that is how he got our attention to correct us. Nothing like being hit in the back of the head with a pebble or a China berry while working on a hot primary. You always had to be ready to get pinged if you weren't doing the right thing. More lessons learned.

A Bad Day

G ene Conger and I were working together. We went in one morning and were assigned a job to cut a set of gang switches in between two 1000 MCM riser poles, so circuits could be switched to give them an alternate feed to some S&C switching cubicles. The customer was Brown and Williamson Tobacco Plant. B&W would have four 2500 KVA transformers serving one building with a single metering point in a row. B&W was a very large customer and viewed as a "critical" customer. Reliability was always an issue. They were a 24-hour-a-day, 7-day-a-week location and never shut down. They made a lot of cigarettes. The job went smooth as silk. We cut the switch in a 750 MCM AAAC conductor circuit hot, kept the new switch jumped out and adjusted the operations so all the blades closed and could be locked properly.

We finished around 2:30 or 3:00 that afternoon. We congratulated each other on a safe job that went well. As we were leaving, we received a call from Dispatch that they had trouble with a 3-phase slack span pull-off near our location. They asked if we could we look at it and take a little slack out of the conductors. The poles had shifted, and the conductors had gotten together in windy conditions and operated the circuit. It was the same circuit we had just cut the switch in on. Naturally, we said, "no problem". The pull-off was at the corner of Cochran Short Route and Weaver Rd, near the new GEICO Insurance office, another important customer. Upon inspecting the pole, we found a 3-phase vertical pull-off to a flat horizontal dead end. I'm not sure who engineered that one but that is another story. The roll from vertical to flat in that short 20' span of wire was the problem. The guys on the flat horizontal dead-end pole were incorrectly installed. The pole was leaning because the guys were not aligned with the conductors properly. The phases had sagged way too close, and any wind would cause them to blow into each other and operate the circuit. Gene and I had looked at it and talked it over with Ed Lunsford, Crew Supervisor that day; John Lane was on vacation. We all decided that the slack span was too slack to even apply a rubber cover on. We decided I would install a split blanket on the slack span insulator sitting vertically on a steel arm. Gene was to hold the phase with his hand to prevent too much vibration as I took the air wrench and loosened the nuts on the slack span clamp. We could then slide the 1/0 primary in the clamp, take up about 6 inches of slack and tighten the clamp back up. That would keep it from cross-phasing again until we could get a switching order in to switch the load, make a permanent correction to the guys, and re-sag all the conductors.

Great plan, but…. I covered the steel arm at the base of the slack span insulator with a 36" X 36" split blanket. I moved the wrench and socket to the nuts on the slack span clamp, because the conductor was so slack it was actually hanging down against the skirts of the insulator. I eased the wrench in place and was watching Gene holding the phase, 7.2 kV, not noticing that the corner of the steel arm was exposed. The wrench contacted the steel, and the entire world turned to fire. A fireball completely engulfed the top of the pole. Guys on the ground could not even see the Hi-Ranger buckets, just the upper booms entering the ball of fire. We also never noticed that whoever framed the horizontal dead-end pole allowed the pole ground to get under the gain on the steel arm. So, when the drill made contact, it was a direct path to neutral—a terrible phase to ground flash. We were five spans from East Macon 115/12kv Substation; we had the breaker on one shot with the reclosing switch disabled. I was told that the breaker operated one time to Instantaneous Lock Out. There were old-style Westinghouse or GE time dial relays set at 0 and 3 seconds, I and T Targets, when in normal operation. We estimated about 8k Amps of fault current at the substation and were only 1000 feet away. The breaker took about eight cycles to clear, but it seemed like two minutes when we were inside the ball of fire. We had no Arc-Rated FR, just a cotton t-shirt that you could almost read a newspaper through, and sunglasses (no ANSI 87.1 UVA or B protection). That was in June of 73', I believe. I can still hear the sound and feel the heat from all those years ago. It made a believer out of me of how crucial proper cover-up is. Even today, many accidents are related to the poor or inadequate cover-up of energized distribution. The insufficient cover-up is a direct cause of violations of the Minimum Approach. The one thing that puzzled me for years (until I met Hugh Hoagland and started working for him after retirement presenting Arc Flash Training), was that I wasn't burned worse. I had a minor second-degree burn between the cuff of my rubber glove and the bottom of the sleeve of my t-shirt. I had a first-degree burn on the right side of my face. The retinas in my eyes suffered minor burns, but the sunglasses kept the glass and metal out of my eyes. I had porcelain fragments embedded in my chest and stomach because I received the brunt of the flash. Gene was to my right and did not get as much of the fireball as I did. I learned much later in my career that distance is inversely proportional to the heat and energy levels in Arc Flash. The worst flash was not at the drill and arm but 5' away, where the ground wire contacted the gain on the steel arm. The 8 k Amps of fault current vaporized the #6 copper for several feet down the pole toward the neutral. It was then I realized that the flash was far enough away, that I did not receive the maximum amount of Arc Flash available. If there was 8-10 Cal at 18", I only had a quarter of the total open-air arc flash because of the distance to the gain. It was bad enough, but the flash could have set my clothes on fire and seriously injured Gene and I. I learned more than one lesson that day. I have kept those memories inside my head since and I'm now determined to share my mistakes so that we can prevent similar events from happening in the future. The fact that we had just completed a highly complex task and finished it with no issues contributed to my and Gene's lack of attention on this job. We were focusing so much on the obvious (the slack span), that we failed to get the bigger picture. I believe the lack of focus and attention to detail plays a significant role in many accidents today. I learned that there is a decrease in attention immediately after completing a difficult and complicated task and we should all realize that that lack of attention can get us in trouble on what might appear to be a simple task.

THINGS THAT HAPPENED

There are many stories about the characters I worked with in Macon all those years. I will share a few I remember as a young Lineman. One day, Tommy Lee came in and wasn't feeling well. He went to get a line truck parked across the driveway, in the storage garage, where all the pulling equipment and air compressors were kept, along with blocks and other materials. Tommy got in the truck and put the transmission in Drive, rather than Reverse. A reason we should back into spaces when arriving, I guess. He drove through the back wall of the garage, into the employee parking lot. It sounded horrible. Unfortunately for me, he missed my pickup, which was parked two parking spaces away from where he went through the wall! I almost got a new truck that day. Tommy was involved in a wreck sometime later that nearly killed him. He was crossing Eisenhower Parkway and pulled in front of a tractor-trailer truck, running the speed limit. I'm not sure if the big rig ran the traffic light. Tommy was only a mile from Key Street Operating. He was lucky that day. Another day, Aubrey Randall was driving a line truck around the transformer rack, out by the pole pile at Key Street Operating, and struck the I-beam supporting the overhead crane we used for loading transformers. We never could figure that one out. The transformer rack was on the opposite corner of the office, but the sound of the digger derrick truck hitting the transformer rack could be heard all over the complex.

As Bill Hammock said, there was a large thunderstorm, or "trash floater", that went through Dublin, Georgia one afternoon, and the number of trouble calls was more significant than the resources in

Dublin. They only had two trouble men and a small line crew. A few were on vacation and unavailable, so the Dublin office called Macon for some help. We loaded all the linemen and apprentices that we could and headed the 60 miles down I-16 to Dublin. We split up and started picking up primaries and changing the transformers from lightning strikes as soon as we got there. We worked steadily until about 2:00 AM. The storms were severe because of a cold front that passed through earlier. We were on some of the last trouble calls in a swampy area, when we heard a radio call that said, "I think it is starting to snow". It was the middle of summer and 100 degrees earlier that day. The cold front did drop the temperature into the 60's or the upper 50's, but there was no snow. He was as serious as he could be. He was working in a swampy bottom with fog. It was cool and clammy after the storm, all the right conditions to make him believe it was snowing.

I remember one storm because it started with Bill and George being the linemen, with myself as Apprentice. We were called in to change a bad transformer. It was about 7:00 PM, Mid-August, and over 100 degrees that day. Before we got that transformer changed out, the Trouble man had called in at least two more. We were also still catching the lights-out calls from overloaded transformers. We had no one to deliver the new transformers, so we went to the "hole" and loaded what we thought we needed: one of the types we knew had burned up and two more 37.5 KVAs in the material trailer and back-of-the-line truck. We had one transformer that had oil still boiling in the tank, so we left that one to cool off and changed one of the others. We wound up changing about six or seven that night, if I remember right. One of them was on a street off Columbus Road in West Macon. I was operating the line truck, while one of the linemen was in a bucket. It was a Friday night, and I think I may have been the only one on the crew that could pass a sobriety test when we were originally called in. It was still about 85-90 degrees after dark, and we were burning up and sweating. Not a dry spot could be found on either of us. We finally got the bad transformer down and the new one installed and connected.

When the lineman closed the switch, a lady came out of her house, screaming that her TV was on fire. Other neighbors could be heard hollering, "Turn it off!". I thought to myself, "Oh no, what have we done?". I know that the data tag on the transformer was the correct size and voltage. The secondary bus on the pole was "Open Route" on a three-spool rack. When the transformer had been removed and the low side disconnected, the lineman in the bucket did not notice the neutral was in the middle position on the rack. When he reconnected the low side, the neutral and top hot leg had been reversed. There were areas in Macon where the neutral was still in the middle position, rather than the top conductor, and this happened to be one of those locations. With the mix-up connecting the low side leads to the transformer, 240 volts and been applied to everything in all of the houses on this transformer. All the 120-volt appliances were being burned up quickly. There were about seven services on that one transformer. I do not know how much that incident cost the company, but it was another lesson learned for me. This is a prime example of being hot and tired while performing redundant tasks and making big mistakes. No job briefings were required back then, so assumptions were made that this transformer would be the same as others. We were not paying attention to anything on the ground before disconnecting the old transformer. We were getting the lights on as fast as we could. Lessons learned are so apparent after the fact: "Plan the job and work the plan".

On the same night, a storm came through around midnight. It was severe enough that we had breaker lockouts all over Macon District. Byron, Georgia (just South of Macon), was fed out of a substation on Hwy 49, just north of Byron. The area was loaded with pecan trees, the "self-trimming tree," as we called them. The storm severely damaged many trees there. The three-phase line feeding Byron was radial and the entire town was out. The South Macon system operator called us and said we needed to head toward the substation because the breaker was locked out. We had just unloaded the last burned-up transformer. We loaded additional material and headed south, to Byron. The three of us (and others that were called in) worked all night long, finally getting off around noon the next day, after working all the previous day and all night long. There were no other incidents during that storm.

Jerry Kirkwood, Rusty Wade, and I were working on a large UD subdivision. One day, we had two Ditch Witch Trenchers digging all at once. Rusty Wade was on an older R 40 and Jerry was on the R 6510. We loved that big, old trencher with rear steering. I was pulling out wire and putting it in the ditch, as the trenchers dug. I heard a noise that I knew did not sound right. I looked around, and Rusty was bouncing on the R 40 like a rubber ball. The noise coming from the digging chain was awful, metal to metal. I ran over and stopped him and asked what was up. Rusty said it was a rock, or just hard ground. I got him to raise the boom to investigate the trench. He had about completely dug through a 48" corrugated steel storm drain. Rusty had not been on the UD crew long and was unfamiliar with the equipment. The company did not pay someone to repair these types of things back then. I had to go to the Cherokee Pipe and Culvert Pipe company to buy a repair band, dig the damaged storm drain metal pipe, and get the band around the pipe to repair it. It may or may not still be there, but we repaired it without additional help. Rusty learned a lesson, and so did I: never let a brand-new WTO operate without oversight until they get some experience.

PROOF TESTED

I was in Macon Ga recently and drove by Ocmulgee Substation to just see if a project Jerry and I worked on back in about 1980 was still there. There was a 'beautification Project" around Central City Park in Macon which included removing two Overhead Feeders out of Ocmulgee Sub and putting them underground. There was one circuit that went straight down Seventh Street, and the other circuit made a right turn out of the Substation and headed North up Lower Riverside Drive. Cecil Brown had gotten with engineering, and it was decided to install parallel runs of 1000 MCM in concrete-encased duct lines for about 500' on each of the feeders. So, we dug the ditches, installed the 6' conduit, poured the concrete installed two brand-new UD riser poles. The substation crews had built us two frames just outside of the breaker bays inside the fence to pull the cable to. Once everything was in place, we assembled a large group of extra help to pull all the cables in. We had to get a 45' Flatbed Low boy and load the large reels of 1000 MCM on to get to the substation. Jerry was in hog heaven since he operated all the equipment by opening the ditches and pulling the cable. Once the cable was in, we had two riser poles with 6 cables to terminate and phase on each Riser Pole and 12 on the frame in the Substation. This was a huge project, and I was privileged to be a part of this installation and termination. When the heavy-duty part of the job was done, the cables were in place, Jerry and I were only left with the task to terminate, phase and mark all cables to be prepared to tie to old conductors and energize. It took a little while to terminate 24 1000 MCM Risers. We were using taped Secroniel stress cones back

then which were fairly new and not using the old, molded stress cones.
We finished after a few days of terminating and the OH crews came to
switch out each circuit, cut the dead ends to new poles, and switch in
the UD Cables. All went well, with no incident, and all was completed
and energized. Jerry and I were very proud of what we were able to do
to be successful in this project. The terminations were just as I had left
them 50 years ago. Wow, that impressed me. My work had outlived its
Warranty! Makes an old Lineman feel good to see his work still active
after all those years. Skilled Labor!

There was another case of a bad three-phase transformer at the
Georgia Farm Bureau at Riverside Drive and Pierce Avenue. Ernie
Campbell and I were called in that night to replace a 300 KVA 120/208
transformer. It turned out to be another learning experience for us.
Ernie and I worked the job as we would any other. It was a radial feed,
no loop, so we picked up a 300 KVA and a line truck to change it out.
All went well on the job. All switches were open, and phases grounded
at the riser pole; it had four runs of 500 MCM on the secondary side.
We taped all the secondaries together, removed the elbows and bushings,
disconnected all grounds, lifted the old transformer out, and installed
the new one. We then connected the grounds, attached the secondary
cables, and plugged all elbows. Ernie and I were both very particular
about tagging and marking cables. We ensured the cables were properly marked before we disconnected everything. All phases reached
back OK. We verified with the maintenance man at the building that
he had opened the main disconnect inside. We removed the grounds,
closed the riser pole cutouts, and checked the voltage. It was perfect:
120 across and 208 between all phases. We told building maintenance
to close the main disconnect and check everything out. A few minutes
later, a maintenance employee came out and asked me to come in so
he could show me something. I went in and discovered that the rotation from the new transformer had been reversed. Oops! I went back
to the transformer and told Ernie, and we started looking, finding what
had happened. The old transformer and the new one had reversed the

phasing on the primary side. The "H1A" phase was on the bottom of the old transformer but on top of the new one. We could not change the primary without splicing, so we swapped X1 and X3 on the load side to reverse and correct the rotation. It worked and we learned that some older transformers had reversed phase rotation. All the newer transformers are now the same, with H1A on top and H3A on the bottom. The older transformer at the Farm Bureau had been there for years, and for whatever reason, H1A and H3A were reversed.

I was still a Lead Lineman on Underground, and Larry McNally was the Foreman. I had several WTOs come and go during this time. I remember Roosevelt "Rosie" Coleman. He was a giant, jovial man that was just fun to work with. He never had a bad day and always made light of everything in life. We were working in a subdivision in Bibb County, trenching in new primary cable, when my attorney called me and informed me that, after a rocky road for several months, my divorce was final. Rosie looked at me and told me that I was finally "disengaged". We both laughed and went back to work. My divorce from Kim's mother was an awful time that I thought I would never get over. After nine years of marriage, I lost everything. The divorce took an entire year, wrangling over assets and who would pay what. I had nothing left. I lost a lovely home and family, and I had to pay off all the bills. June and I started out together in a mobile home. By the time the divorce occurred, we had bought and sold several times and were living in the house in Lizella. After the divorce, I rented a small house near the office, in Hillcrest Heights. I worked every minute of overtime I could, in order to pay off all the bills, and move on with my life. After a while, I recovered financially, and then I met Vicki.

Jerry Kirkwood was my WTO, and I was still on the UD crew. We were a two-man crew and I had to call in my own UD requests for the location of utilities. My crew caught most of the bad cables and other trouble calls. I called in my locates as needed, most being "Emergency Locates". Our main concern was telephone and gas lines. I had a Dynatel 573P, allowing me to locate almost anything I needed and not wait on other locators. Individual companies had their employees locating their facilities, rather than a One Call service like we have today. We became good friends with most utility locators. I kept their phone numbers handy. Back then, I had a telephone handset to where I could find a Bell Pedestal, find a phone line that was not in use, and just call the locators directly. Southern Bell had a phone number connected to their radio system, so I could call them on radios or phones. One Bell South cable repair employee often located Bell cables for us, JL "Jimmy" Dartez. He was unique, Cajun by ethnicity, and so fun to talk to. If you tied his hands behind his back, he was unable to say a word. I had to wait for a location to be completed sometimes because JL would stop for a coffee break in the middle of a job. JL had located cable for us for years and never mentioned that he had a daughter.

VICK DARTEZ

I met Vicki <u>Dartez</u> at Northside Bowling Center while working a part-time job there during the year IBEW LU 84 was on strike because of a Labor and Benefits disagreement. Vicki had come in to meet one of the other employees because she had broken up with a boyfriend and a friend of hers, Carolyn Handley, wanted her to meet this other guy. I melted when she walked through the door with Carolyn. Carolyn's husband, Sonny Handley, also a Bell South employee, was friends with JL Dartez, Vicki's Dad. I had been divorced a year or so, living a bachelor's life, and was ready for a permanent relationship. As soon as we talked for a bit, she called her Dad to ask if he knew Danny Raines at GPC. His response was, "Is he a fat boy?". Vicki did not tell me that story until much later in our relationship. Small world. Vicki's Mom and Dad and my Mom and Dad were all married on Christmas Day. Vicki and I met in August and married on Christmas Day that same year. The strike ended after a few weeks with a settlement, and we all returned to work. The strike resulted in a change in health benefits and a whopping 1% salary increase. The best benefit of that strike was meeting Vicki. Here we are, over 40 years later! Still together with Children and Grand Children. Vicki is also the "Bonus Mom" to my oldest Daughter, Kim, two Granddaughters, and now two Great Grand Children.

MEANWHILE BACK ON THE CREW

We were following behind a contractor that had been installing cable. Jerry and I would terminate the transformers as the contractor completed a section at a time. It was a three-phase circuit extension from a shorter loop feed. The load was split between the three primaries, and there were no radial taps so it would be a three-phase loop, a huge subdivision with large houses on 2-acre lots, or larger. There were many terminations. The design included many terminating cabinets on the property lines at the road with a single-phase primary down the property line with a transformer and services to two houses. This required verifying many cables, tagging, and ringing out for correct phasing and marking. I loved that kind of project. Jerry and I worked several subdivisions like this on the north side of Macon, with total electric houses and with a lot of load. Great care was taken to balance the load on the three UD primaries, so when we made up the UD Risers to overhead, the load would be balanced on the OH system. On this job, Jerry and I found several splices that had not been made as the contractors installed the cable and would come to the end of a reel. They would start a new section and backfill and cover up the ends of the two cables without notifying GPC that they needed a splice. Jerry and I would walk out the cables from one transformer or TC Cabinet to the next termination and suddenly discover an open cable. We had a Thumper, so we would set up and perform the fault locating and find the open, dig a splice pit, and complete that part of the loop. It didn't take long for GPC to figure out they needed a turn-key job and not to let one crew dig and another terminate.

When we finally got ready to start switching in the new sections where the initial was stopped, a temporary tie was put under the road to maintain a "loop fed" system. I started writing the switching order. It was a very long, but not complicated three-phase loop. The normal open points had been assigned by engineering on all three phases at different locations in the subdivision. The plan was to maintain service to all homes without outages while switching to the new section. Larry McNally, our Foreman, took one look at the switching order and just left. He did not want anything to do with it so that he would not get the blame if something went wrong. His words to me were, "Handle it, Bye!".

Another time, Larry had started another three-phase subdivision, off Rivoli Drive, and had to trench all three phases down to what was going to be a two-transformer Delta Bank on UD, to feed a sewage lift pump. Larry and Roosevelt built it to the pump and then continued to a terminating cabinet to stop for a short time until the road was completed, and the three-phase loop could be continued. The job was to get all three phases hot to the 2-pot Delta Bank and continue the three phases to a TC Cabinet next to the Delta bank. His crew had worked all week to get to the cabinet and get the bank hot. They did just that. They set a Single-Phase TC Cabinet as a "temporary" stopping point, and when they terminated all the phase conductors in the TC Cabinet, all three phases were put on a three-way feed-through. They completed all the tagging of phases, double-checked everything back to the three-phase riser pole, and closed all three phases. Nothing happened (that was noticed) at that point. But what really happened was, when they closed the second switch, it locked out a pole recloser down Rivoli Drive. Then they closed the third switch and locked out a second breaker. So, now one breaker was feeding all of Rivoli Drive beyond the three pole reclosers. It was feeding down the new subdivision and back out to the switches on the riser pole. The load was not too great at the time, so the 100-Amp breaker was carrying the load. All was fine until a customer with a three-phase service called to report a single phasing condition. There were no other lights-out calls coming in. I was on the trouble truck that day and got to the customer first. There was no blown fuse on the bank. I immediately checked the reclosers and found two locked out. That did not make any sense, since no other trouble calls were reported. We had heard that the new subdivision had just been made hot, so we headed that way first. We opened the risers to de-energize, went back to the reclosers, and made the breakers hot. They held! Not sure who first noticed, but by the time I got back to the subdivision and started checking, it dawned on us that there was a single-phase cabinet at the end of the three-phase line. It should have three single-phase parking stands. We opened it up and found all three phases on the three-way feed-through and BINGO! A three-phase dead short and cross phase with no flash. Just locked out each single-phase breaker till the fault was cleared. McNally and his crew had a tough time living that one down. Everybody gave "Mr. McNally" a hard time for a while!

There were days we did not have enough orders to keep us busy all day. Jerry and I knew where the active subdivisions were, so we would ride them daily. We would find a house that was framed up and did not have a meter base up yet, but we could tell where the entrant cable was to be run out the wall. We would run the service and stub it out at a temporary pole or transformer and against the house, leaving it ready to splice or leave off on a transformer. We would have no order, so we would draw up a print, shoot the angles with a compass and measure the length of the service to draw an image and account for the service conductor. We would then turn the sketch for engineering to change maps. The engineers loved it. They never went to subdivisions after the primaries were made hot and everything was in except the services. I think we may have been serving two purposes then. I guess that was my way of "running a spare", that I learned from Albert Smith. I can remember days when this sure came in handy. We might have orders to set several meters in one day, and if it were not for the spares we ran, we could not have finished and made everyone happy. If we were lucky, the electrician would put it in the pipe and leave the service hanging out of the meter base. The only hard time we had was when the developers of a subdivision would split a lot and make two lots from one. Then, we had no stub out for the new lot. A "Y" splice would be needed, and that could be a major headache. A bad hot leg on either of the services beyond the "Y" splice was challenging to repair. You better have good prints or nasty things happen to a house when not disconnected from the Hypotronics Thumper looking for the bad spot. Yes, that has happened.

Jerry and I worked together for several years. Jerry loved to get Snickers candy bars whenever we stopped for a break, or at a store for a drink. He ate two or three large candy bars a day! We worked well together and put a lot of wire in the ground. One day, we had to dig a service to a large house in Lake Wildwood. Jerry got the R-6510 Ditch Witch stuck in a low place, and I had to get on a backhoe and use it to push us out of the bog hole while Jerry was trying to back us up. I pushed the front of the trencher up high to get the front tires out of the mud and tried to back up. The bolts that held the seat broke, and I fell back against the muffler and exhaust pipe. I received a nasty burn through my shirt. Jerry had the throttle wide open, so it was hot as Hades! The design of the exhaust system changed, and a shroud was put over the existing mufflers to add a guard from the extreme heat.

There was a competition between the linemen when it came to underground work. Cecil Brown was still a Cable Splicer on the Network Crew when the Macon Mall began being built. Charlie Tidwell and Ernie Campbell were declared as leads on the Mall Loop Circuit. We had just begun setting S&C switching cubicles with vaults. Charlie Tidwell became the "Keeper of the Keys" for the mall installation and installed some of the first cubicles. We installed several cubicles at the Macon Mall and all over the Division and District. One morning, I was on the loading dock near what was fondly referred to as the "Idiot Bench", where we all sat in the mornings, waiting to go to work. David Williamson dubbed Charlie Tidwell the "Wizard of UD", since he was the mall guy. The Idiot Bench exploded with laughter. The same happened when Bennie Arnold called Cecil Brown "Banana Foot", since he wore a size 14 shoe.

Charlie Tidwell had an opportunity to interview for a supervisor position down south, in the Macon Division. Charlie parked his truck inside the fence to secure it while in the interview. He knew it would be late when he got back. Seeing his truck and knowing what he was doing was all it took for a trick to be played on the Wizard. I will not name the culprits here, but there were several! When Charlie returned after the interview, he got in his truck to leave, cranked it up, and put it in Drive. Nothing happened. The truck's rear had been raised, blocks of cross arms were placed under spring shackles on the truck, and the tires were about an inch off the ground. Charlie had to get a line truck to lift the pickup and remove the blocks. My gosh, those were the days.

There was a piece of automatic switch gear called a Vacpac that was installed at commercial buildings that wanted an "uninterruptable" service. Rather than install a spot network, a VacPac would be installed with a two-way feed from two different feeders and substations. The VacPac could be set up with preferred and alternate feeders. It had PTs and CTs for monitoring and metering. Still, if the feeder on the preferred source operated, the VacPac would go to the Alternate feed and stay for a length of time to ensure the preferred circuit was back in normal operations. The VacPac would tie the substation breakers for a few cycles and not affect regulators' operations at the substations. It was amazing technology for the 70's. The automatic switching was so fast that if you were on an elevator, you never knew when the VacPac would switch from Alternate to Preferred or back.

One location with a VacPac had a lightning strike that damaged the VacPac. After repairs were made and power was restored, we megged the grounds at the riser poles. We discovered that the ground resistance was extremely high, over 2000 Ohms in many cases. Lightning arrestors work best at a low ground resistance. NESC suggests 25 Ohms or less, which is very difficult to obtain. Cecil Brown started a maintenance program, checking all the riser poles and driving additional ground rods. Jerry Kirkwood and I took the brick truck and an air compressor around to all the riser poles and started megging pole grounds. This program went on during the winter months when Capital work was slow. I have no idea how many bundles of ground rods we drove, but there were many. I can remember driving as many as 20 rods on one pole when the soil was sandy, and resistance was high.

All of us linemen had scary moments at one time or another and thank goodness none of us were ever really injured. I had locked out the breaker on 7th Street using the tape to secure a 750 MCM jumper, Carl Leslie put a mechanical jumper from Phase 1 to Phase 3 on a junction pole on College Street and cross-phased 12.4 kV. Gene conger and I had a flash from inadequate cover on Cochran Short Route, four spans from a substation. Before we started spiking cables on UD, I was working on a Saturday outage, extending another one of those "temporary" stops on a UD Circuit. Someone had cut in a new transformer and had not changed cable tags. We had to cut cables and reroute to the new transformer. I was told the cable had been switched out and was "dead" (nothing is ever dead), so I cut an energized 7.2 kV primary while in the hole with it. Boy, I had a fire in my face! Then the switch blew a 50-amp KS fuse close to us, and between the arc on the primary and the fuse blowing, I almost had a heart attack. Many of us could have been killed or burned many times, but we were not. This may explain why I strongly recommend following all the rules, all the time. The rules are written and are in place because of the mistakes and discoveries of the past.

On another occasion, I was helping Ed Lunsford strip out a double dead end with a double set of wood arms. The middle phase was a dead end on the through bolt of the wood arms rather than an eye bolt above the arms. I was on the back side of the pole and started removing the hardware, taking my air wrench, and removing the nuts off the back side of the arms to remove the arm. I removed the lock nuts and nuts off the DA bolt on the end and moved to the through for the arm at the pole. When I removed the lock nut and nut, the bolt pulled through the pole with the weight of the phase conductor (which was 1/0 Copper), and shot straight out, falling into the neutral mid-span. Phase to ground, 7.2 kV to neutral about 100' out in span, locked out the breaker. Another "oops" with nothing but embarrassment for me and another lesson learned. I am airing out a lot of "dirty laundry", but I hope it's all a lesson about how easy it is to make mistakes. I look back and realize many of my mistakes were a lack of communication with Ed on the other side of the pole. I did not see that the phase was dead-ended on the arm bolt. Ed asked me to strip the arms out, and away I went. He thought I had seen the screw eye on the arm bolt holding the middle phase. I have seen grounds left on UD Pad mount transformers, and overhead primary pull-offs, and experienced linemen attempt to reenergize them and blow fuses. They would stop and say, "What happened?", and then we would all stand around and ask, "Why did I let that happen?". When I look back on the stupid things myself and others did, and the fact that job briefings were not required (or even considered) back then, it is a wonder that any of us made it out alive. It is also obvious why a job briefing is crucial to the safety of the job and the employees. I have investigated many accidents where the lack of an adequate job briefing was the root cause of the accident.

Ed and I were given a junction pole to change out one day. A transmission pole, three spans out of the substation, in Payne City, a mill village within the city of Macon. We had gone to look at the pole a day or so before and saw it would be a challenge. Ed and I loved tough jobs because they make a good lineman even better. The pole was a 4-way dead-end junction pole. It had the main feeder circuit out of Substation, 4/0 Copper, a three-phase pull-off on the third side that fed a milk dairy, and a single phase on the fourth side that continued down the street. We could not get an outage on any part of the circuit since it was so close to the substation, and the dairy was a 24-hour continuous operation. We had to keep it all hot. The road was widened, so the pole was shifted back about 12' or so. We had to use 4/0 mechanical jumpers on the main circuit, 20' long. We call them "anacondas" because they are so big and heavy. We used 1/0 jumpers on the three-phase pull-off to the dairy and single-phase pull-off down Brookdale Avenue, toward Payne City. We started at daylight the day of the transfer and knew it would be a long day. The transmission crew had set the pole, and the 115 kV transmission line had been transferred to the new pole. We had to move the 12 kV distribution to the new pole. It's no easy task keeping everything hot and moving that far back, but by 4:00 that afternoon, it was done. John Lane was the Foreman, and everything went as planned that day. Ed was a great planner and taught me so much about line work and common sense, as I stumbled through the first year or so as a Lineman.

MORE EXPERIENCES

I was providing a safety meeting on system grounding recently, and I mentioned OSHA in the presentation. One of the linemen said, "OSHA Sucks". I immediately reminded him that OSHA Regulations are minimum rules for safety, based solely on events like what I am recounting in this book. Employees do not understand and are not trained on the "why" behind the regulations that are written—one set of rules for every system in the USA. Delta or Wye-Wye does not matter. Regulations do not explain how to work on an Electric Utility system. The regulations tell the "why and what", and employers must determine the "how" to perform the task and stay within the rules and regulations. Therefore, I have dedicated my career to helping workers understand the "why" behind the "what". Workers need to understand the importance of a rule and what is in it for them to follow the regulation. Simply being told, "that is the rule" never works for anyone, especially line workers.

This reminds me of a time when I was called in on a broken pole. The pole was a three-phase C-suspension pole on Hwy 247, south of Macon, toward the Middle Georgia Regional Airport. I was a blue slipped Apprentice to Lineman that night. We arrived on the scene; it was an awful wreck with severe injuries. The victims had been taken to the hospital, and the car was removed from the scene. The pole was a 50' Class 3, because the three-phase circuit crossed the four-lane road with a median. The wire was down everywhere, and police blocked the road on either side of the accident. All lanes were closed. It was about 2:00 AM, so traffic was light. There was a sense of urgency to get the pole in and wire it up before the Warner Robins Air Force Base traffic started leaving Macon, heading south to the base. Once the accident was clear of all civilians, we set up a work zone and went to work. We had no problem picking up the broken pole, digging a new hole, and setting the 50' pole. We framed the new pole with two down guys on the backside and three sets of discs insulators on eye bolts for the three-phase conductors. The C-pole was in the center of two poles with cross arms just below and across the road. "Cherokee" Joe Wood and I installed the conductors as our spec book required. Inside of the angle to the bottom, the "B" phase to the top, and the outside phase to the middle. We were able to pick everything up and were ready to remove the grounds and re-energize at about 4:00 AM. Once that was completed, we called the System Operator and dispatched a switching order to "make it hot". All went well, so we were picking up all the material and the broken pole to take back in. The Operator called us and said to meet a maintenance person at a plant down the road because there was a problem. Once we contacted the maintenance guy, we discovered rotation had been reversed. That was confusing because we knew we had built it back as the spec book required. The phase numbers were not on a pole at the accident location, so we went down the road to a three-phase riser UD Pole where the phases were marked and discovered the problem. Back in the day, before GPC changed to what is now in the spec book on how to turn an angle pole, the "Airplane" turn was sometimes used. "B" Phase would be in the middle position on vertical construction rather than in the top position on the pole. We figured out that this broken C-pole had an airplane turn, and when we replaced the pole and built it back to current specs, we reversed the rotation on primary locations. We had to go back to the accident pole, energize and ground again to move the "B" phase to the middle position. Now, it was 6:00 AM, rush hour had started, people going to work at the Air Force Base were aggravated, and this Apprentice had learned another valuable lesson in verifying phases and rotation at the expense of the victims of the car wreck. The making of a Lineman.

After all the years of walking in yards, in all hours of night and day, I was only bitten by a dog once. It happened in Stockbridge, Georgia, during an ice storm in 1982, at about 1:00 AM, and it was by a small Cocker Spaniel. I wore a rain suit and overalls, and the teeth never broke the skin. This was the same ice storm that caused me to leave my new bride to go on storm trouble. Vicki and I got married on Christmas Day (just like my parents and her parents had). Only a few weeks after that, Jonesboro had an ice storm, and away I went. It had been cold and rainy in Macon, but no ice. Vicki had made a massive pot of beef stew, cold weather comfort food as I called it. About the time she finished the stew, I was called to go and left her alone at home. I was gone for three days on storm duty, and she ate beef stew every day I was gone. She will hardly make it today, some 40 years later—the life of a lineman's wife.

I walked in a driveway once and found a Great Dane in an old, abandoned station wagon, which was his "doghouse". I almost had a heart attack on that one. He was as quiet as a church mouse until I was a few feet away from the vehicle. The car was in the shade and the windows were rolled up enough to keep him in. Thank God!

I was a Lead Lineman on Underground Crew in the late '70s. We were about to get off, but got called about a Bad UD Service, one leg dead. Cecil Brown asked for volunteers, so naturally, I jumped on the chance. I recruited James and Ken Wall, and we rolled out to North Macon. Hugh Wright was the Trouble man that first answered the partial light call. He warned me about a big, black Labrador at the house. He was aggressive. When we pulled up in the UD Brick Truck, the customer was talking to his neighbor in his driveway. I stepped out of the truck, put a hard hat on, and started walking up the driveway—no dog in sight. I was about halfway to the two gentlemen, when the lab came from the back of the house, running straight at me. The dog's owner just stood there and never said a word. I looked back at the truck and realized there was no way I could outrun the dog. I turned around, ran at the dog, and timed it perfectly with a drop kick straight to his nose and chin. It may have broken the dog's jaw, I'm not sure. The dog ran the other way and I fell flat on my behind because I had kicked it so hard. The dog's owner never said a word; they just stood there. I wanted to kick him. Why people do things like that, I never will know.

Gary Jackson was on the southside Cut-In truck once and walked into a business that was a TV Repair store. They had a "Junk Yard Dog" as security that attacked Gary. He very calmly grabbed the dog's jaws and snapped them back, breaking the jaw. The owner stood there watching and did not say a word until the episode was over. He then complained and filed a loss suit for the dog. I learned to never trust a customer's dog when it goes into a "defensive" mode with the owner present. That is what is to be expected. When the dog's owners or family appear, they change their presence. Be ready.

The linemen on the three Cut-In trucks were typically Senior Linemen and very dedicated to their jobs. Albert Smith was on Westside; Bennie Britt was on Eastside; John Lane was on Southside. I remember Albert Smith lost his billfold one day in the locker room, when he went to the bathroom, and it had several hundred dollars in it. Not sure who found it and gave it back to him, but that was how we were in those days. I worked with all three as an Apprentice. That was so much fun. Bill Hammock was on the East Side Cut-In filling in one day and had a wreck at Emery Highway and Second Street. It was told that he looked away for a second, when a car in front of him stopped at a green light for no reason, causing him to hit them in the rear. Another lesson learned. Just because the light is green, you should still be very careful. State Law declares, "Drivers can proceed on a green light if the intersection is clear of all traffic and pedestrians". I never will forget that. Later in my career, I was a Smith Driver Improvement Instructor, and that thought was always in the back of my mind when teaching a driver class.

MORE STORMS AND TROUBLE

C ecil Brown was Team Leader on a storm in the Carolinas and led an "A" Team (a large group with supporting staff of tree crews and garage mechanics). The team also included a few logistics and administrative employees for the team, to find food, hotels, and laundry. As time went on, the storm teams changed considerably. More support staff was added, so the crews could work more. When I first went into Field Safety, we were part of the Advanced Team that went ahead of the crew convoy. A group of us would be first to the staging area to receive all the "marching orders" from the host company, find hotels, obtain the line maps of the areas that were to be assigned to the teams, and be ready when the crews arrived. The idea was for the crews to go straight to work upon arrival and have all information needed in order to be more efficient.

It was on another storm that the team was on the way back, we stopped to eat at a steak house somewhere in North Carolina or South Carolina. We had stopped at least once, and they could not serve us because we had too many to feed at once and not enough table space. This restaurant was cafeteria-style, so we went through the line. Bruce "Tater" Peterson was right behind me in line. All I heard was, "I am starving to death". The server took his order, and he ordered two #8's off the menu. The #8 was a rib eye and a baked potato. From then on, Bruce's nickname was "Tater", given to him by Ed Lunsford and Cecil Brown. Bruce did eat both steaks and potatoes and dessert! Bruce was also my last "Pole Buddy" on the Macon Apprentice Training Crew when I was awarded a Supervisor job in Jonesboro in 1985. Bruce had a beautiful family and Pam, his widow, is still friends on Social Media. The family continues

We had a broken pole on one Friday night before the opening day of Deer Season. I was in one bucket, and Lathrope Holder was in another. We had blocked the street off, had a new pole set, and were tying in the conductors. It was about 4:30 AM on Saturday, the opening day of deer season. We heard some shouting and a bang. I thought somebody had another wreck right there in our work zone. I turned and looked down, only to see John Lane climbing off the hood of a pickup truck and snatching a door open, dragging the driver out. The driver had run through all the traffic cones and was drunk. He said he was on the way to the deer camp to go hunting; imagine that. The police showed up and took him in another direction. John was okay; he had jumped on the hood of the drunk guy's truck to keep from getting hit.

Another Friday night before the opening day of deer season, while I was still an Apprentice brings another story. There was a three-phase main line pole hit on Houston Road in South Bibb County. It was torn down to the ground. I'm not sure who the linemen were that night, but Bennie Arnold and I were on the ground. We were getting a 5"X5"X8' wood arm ready to send up the pole. We had the arm laying on the end of the material trailer to install P-6 pins, I-9 insulators, and a pole gain on it. We picked it up and handed it to one of the linemen in a bucket who had dropped down to get the arm. The arm was heavy, it was 2:00 AM, and there was not enough light to see what we were doing. The I-9 hung up on something in the trailer, causing the arm to slip out of my hands. Bennie could not hold on to his end, so he let it go. The arm dropped on his foot and cracked a bone in his instep arch. He never let me live that one down. He missed the opening day of deer season and walked around for a month with a boot on his foot. You don't mess with a man's deer season down south!

Smokie Smarr was Foreman on a crew when we had a pole broken on a bad curve on Rocky Creek Road. It was at night, and there were no streetlights or moon light. We only had some hand lights to work by. The circuit was locked out. Ed Lunsford and I were the Linemen. We had a WTO, an Apprentice, and a Helper. Smokie was always impatient and in a huff most of the time. He kept a cigar in his mouth and was always running around, barking orders. He was walking around the line truck when it had completed digging the hole for the new pole. The auger had been stowed away, and the pole had been raised high enough in a "setting hold" so that we could frame the pole before we set it in place. The pole hole was open and unattended since the crew was busy installing hardware and pole ground on the pole. Smokie was walking quickly around the butt of the pole and suddenly, he was gone. He disappeared and not a sound could be heard for a few seconds. Then, he started fussing and we went looking for him. We found that he had stepped into the unguarded pole hole; Smokie was standing at the bottom of the 6.5' pole hole fuming! Smokie was only about 5'5" tall, so of course, this was a prime opportunity to harass him a bit. We all stood in a circle around the pole hole, with flashlights shining down on him. We made him think we were all about to drain our bladders in the pole hole on him! That's a series of expletives I cannot repeat in this book! Of course, we were joking, but you couldn't pass up opportunities like that. If you wonder why pole holes should be guarded, there are more reasons than to just prevent falls!

There was another incident many years later that I was not involved in. I had presented New Hire Training to the victim before I retired from Georgia Power. He attempted to complete the day by setting a pole without proper locates. If he would have taken the pole back to headquarters and called for locates, he would still be alive today. He decided he could pull the old pole while holding a primary in the material-handling jib of a material-handling bucket truck and float the neutral and communication cables. The crew removed the old pole. They hand-dug it out to where it was about 4 feet or deeper and attempted to use the auger to clean out the hole for the new pole. A gas contractor had installed a 4" gas main underneath the old pole with a directional boring machine. The point of the auger punctured the main, gas started escaping, and as everyone attempted to move back, the movement of the bucket caused the hot phase to create a small arc, igniting the gas. He died in the natural gas fire, and the fire was 20 feet or more from the ground. He could not escape before the bucket and boom burned, killing him. He fell to the ground when the bucket and boom burned and melted. It was a horrible accident and only happened due to the personal initiative of attempting to do a job. Always be safe and never take chances without proper locates. He was trying to do a great job but did not follow the rules and paid the ultimate sacrifice.

Just Glad to Have Been There

The reality is that most all the people I worked with at GPC were genuine "Salt of the Earth" type folks, people you would want to be around. As I am sitting here authoring this book of linemen stories and my career, I just lost a very dear friend of 40 or more years. Wayne Fauscett was a lineman in Gainesville, GA, Northeast Region (once Athens Division). Wayne worked in Safety and Training for years and wound up in Central Region, the old Macon Division, before retiring. Wayne retired about two or three years after I did, and when he retired, I immediately hired him at Raines Utility Safety Solutions, LLC. Wayne was great at accident investigations and audits. Once the dedication of the job sits in, we all want to share our experiences in hopes that they may save someone's life in the future. Wayne was that way, too. The dedication is exactly why I am authoring this book. Another Wayne comes to mind, Wayne Hardin. He is one of the best Distribution Cover Up Trainers ever. He has been working with me for 6 years now and still going.

SIDNEY "RATTLER" BOYD

I made so many friends and acquaintances at Georgia Power. Certain individuals stick in your mind more than others. The faces in the other bucket across from me, that I depended on, and they on me to do the right thing and look out for each other. That was how it was: a family, a brotherhood of tough, rugged guys and a few ladies that I will mention later. We worked long and hard to satisfy the customer and the company. There was a kind of loyalty that is hard to find in other places. Lineman jobs are challenging, and we were all very proud of the type of work and skills needed to perform the tasks that were required of us. A Journeyman Lineman is a unique type of skilled labor. The training methods are better than ever in today's industry. As an Apprentice or young Lineman, we were tossed out there to the real world and learned from our mistakes. Today, there are so many resources to help linemen learn the basics of electricity, how systems work, coordination of protection, and even protective devices like relays that sense and clear faults faster than we can think. No time dials and moving the trip settings of relays by moving the screw for 120 Amp increases. Oh, yes, open the knife blade switches to disable the relay when moving the screw! I digress…

The time I spent in Macon before I bid on and was successfully selected as Crew Foreman/Supervisor in 1985, was indeed a blessing. I worked with great Georgia Power employees during my time there. I came back to Macon on Smokie's Crew. Sidney "Rattler" Boyd made Foreman shortly after I returned from Jonesboro. I worked with Sidney and the crew for several months. John Lane's son, Keith, also came through Macon for a time and worked with Sidney. Keith remains a friend today, even though he left Georgia Power. There were so many stories about Rattler that I could tell. A few are so funny, I must!

Keith Lane reminded me of the time when "the whistler" would get on the company radio and let out a high-pitched whistle every day. The radio system back then was VHF frequencies, and during the summer, we could hear companies all over the United States, mainly up north, talking as if they were local. The radio guys explained environmental conditions that caused the radio signals to skip and bounce everywhere. It may have been one of those guys who started it. It drove Sidney crazy. I have seen him pick up the microphone and tell them to stop it, which only caused it to get worse. The whistling went on for a long time. A trick was played on Sidney once that caused a ruckus, for sure. He almost had a heart attack. Someone, whom I will not identify, went to see Joe in the radio shop at the Riverside Drive office and got an old microphone that had failed and was set to be scrapped. The microphone on the line truck was switched with the old mic that did not work. Later that day, out on the job, Sidney went to call someone on the radio, and they did not answer. He tried several times, said a few choice words, and threw the mic in his seat. Rattler was not aware of the switch, of course. One of the linemen, not to be mentioned, went over to the line truck, took his 9" Kline cutting pliers, and cut the microphone cord. He took the mic, gave it to Sidney, and told him he was tired of this radio and fussing, so now he did not have to listen anymore. Sidney nearly spit his teeth out. We all laughed and then told Sidney what was going on. Of course, Sidney did not think it was funny, but no one cared.

I was not present at the time when Sidney was a lineman changing a junction pole out at the intersection of Bloomfield Road and Rocky Creek Road. The pole was a flat double wood arm dead-end with a 90-degree left turn. Sidney was in a bucket; I'm not sure who was in the other bucket, but it may have been George Aycock. The pole transfer of conductors had been completed, permanent jumpers were made up, and Sidney started removing the mechanical jumpers. Someone looked up and hollered that he had two different mechanical jumpers and two different phases in the bucket with him at the same time. He was just inches away from cross-phasing primaries through him. His only remark was, "That is what you are down there for, to watch me!". Hence the need for a dedicated observer, by today's standards.

There is a street that is part of an intersection at Vineville Avenue, Pio Nono Avenue, and Pierce Avenue in Macon, Georgia, named Stanislaus Circle. When Sydney was on the westside Cut-In truck, we had several re-wires on the houses, upgrading service to accommodate more air conditioning. When they would dispatch a call to the street for either lights out or a re-wire, Sidney would reply with the house number and "Santa Clause Circle". He could never say Stanislaus. He was an absolute hoot when the pronunciation of the English language was in question. He also was notorious for his setting of expectations. He was the Foreman over the UD Crew Jerry Kirkwood, and I were on. When the weather was nice, Jerry and I would go to the brick truck, gas up, fill up the ice keg, and be ready to pull out shortly after 8:00AM. Sidney would meet us in the parking lot with the print of the day if we had one. If we had no large subdivision going on, we could catch a bad service to a house, cut cable, or tend to a streetlight out with a bad or cut UD service conductor. His last words were always, "Go out there and do the best you can for the most. You know what to do; just be careful". That was Sidney. I loved that guy!

THE COLDEST NIGHT

The weather never really had gotten cold in Macon in my career. A 20-degree night was as bad as it had gotten in the past. I remember a January night when it was freezing. I was called in to catch trouble, with everyone else they could call in, because poles were breaking, and wire was falling everywhere. The temperature had gotten down to -5 degrees. All the bad habits of the past became known that day. No one used sagging tables or Dynamometers back then and they learned a lesson or two about why it was so important. The trucks would hardly operate because the hydraulic fluid had gotten so cold. Of course, we were so cold we had to stop to get warmed up every few minutes. None of us had ever seen anything like this. Johnny Bell and I were toward Byron on Cornfield Road. We received a call saying the breaker was locked out and the wire was on the ground. We thought that the 750 MCM that was pulled in recently by contractors sagged too tight. We pulled up on the scene and sure enough, a set of 1200 Amp gang switches was torn apart, and all the primaries were on the ground. There were some, back in the day, that loved seeing wire pulled in and sagged tight. Conductors were sagged much tighter than they should have been. The old saying was, "get all you can, then what you are going to lose and make it up". Sagged probably at about 1500-2000 pounds, it looked good in 90-degree weather. We had to splice wire to get back in dead-end shoes and cut the gang switches out until it warmed up. Johnny was stripping the pole to get the gang switches out and I saw him about to pull a cotter key from a set of bells to put it in his mouth, just as we always did when it was warm. That was a bad idea this night. The cotter key was frozen and the key stuck to his lips! He pulled all the meat right off his lips when he pulled the key off. I hollered not to do it, but it was too late, and the damage was done. His entire lip and part of his tongue had frozen to cotter key. That left more than a bruise.

We had another trouble call on Mosley Dixon Road, out by Lake Tobesofkee, that a pole was broken. The crew arrived on the scene, and all three primaries and the pole were lying on the ground, in the road. The conductors were 397 MCM and had also been sagged too tight. All the conductors and hardware were laying across the road. The wire should have been sagged at about 1200 pounds in both cases. When installed, it was sagged at over 2000 pounds. It was so cold that night, with the conductors sagged too tight, the 4" curved washers on the down guy fittings pulled through the pole. So, the hardware would not hold the strain when the aluminum wire contracted due to cold temperatures.

EARL GRANT

J ust down the road from this location, another significant change was occurring. Echoconee Substation was being built because the city Byron was growing. The customer load was rising faster than the current system could handle and more was expected. The nearest substation was back at the airport, some 10 miles away. A 115 kV transmission line extending down to the new substation from Middle Georgia Regional Airport Station, on Griffin Rd. The new line was constructed, except for crossing the big intersection of the two highways. The Macon Transmission Crew was completing the last span into the substation from a vertical dead end of the 115 kV line across the intersection. The pole was a 100' Class 1. Earl Grant was working on the crew, hanging off conductors to be pulled across the road. Earl was at the top of the 100' pole, attaching the static wire and "cutting out" with one hook, as he moved around the pole. Time stood still for a second, and everyone on the ground just froze in position when he started to fall; Earl was able to catch himself and get the hook back in the pole without incident. I look back on those things and understand completely why "free climbing" is not the safest thing we could do. Granted, it was viewed to be a "rite of passage", when you recognized a "qualified" Apprentice/Lineman.

FREE CLIMBING

When I was a "Guest Instructor", teaching Apprentice Training in Macon, there was a 75' 115 kV "H" Structure across the street from the office. We used that structure to confirm the climbing abilities of new apprentices. At that time, new apprentices were expected to "free climb" to the spar arm of the 75' structure to "pass the class". I climbed to the spar arm, took my safety off, climbed up on, and sat on the Spar Arm to watch the class climb up and back down, many times. It was fun to see who could and watch the ones that had doubts. It was not hard to determine. I would encourage them and reassure them that they could make it. Most did. Occasionally, one would wash out and not make it. It did not happen often though. By this time, they had figured it out.

Learning as We Went

When installing a new Underground Distribution System in a new Subdivision, we would stub services out energized in a 2" stub out PVC pipe. That way we felt that if anyone would dig into the service and cut it, they would report that to the company. That worked well until the economy caused the construction of new houses to stop so which left many building lots vacant for many months, sometimes years. Mowing crews cutting right of way would cut down the conduits and expose the energized conductors. If they hit it just right, they could cut the service in two, and short them out. This meant that there would be a 120/240-volt service exposed to anyone that walked by. There was one occasion, I remember, where a customer's daughter, about 12 years old, ran to the edge of their yard to get a ball, stepped on the service, and burned her foot and leg. From that point on, we never stubbed another service out hot. We spent weeks identifying and disconnecting hot stub outs. More lessons learned!

I worked on the three-man crews until an Apprentice Training Crew was started for the Macon division in the mid-eighties. I bid on, interviewed, and was selected to be a Crew Leader. Charlie Hilton supervised the Training Crew, I was the crew leader, Bruce Peterson was the lineman, and we had three Apprentice Trainees. We sat down and developed a written test for entry, to see what level of experience each new Apprentice had, so we could pinpoint the areas that needed the most attention. The first few days were spent on the low line training field, learning to tie in conductors and frame poles. Finally, Apprentices were allowed in bucket trucks, to build transformer installation, sag conductors, and finally start working on energized conductors and equipment. By the time the Apprentices made it to the Training Crew they had their "feet wet" by the crews they had come from. The crew, foremen, and linemen occasionally let them work the bucket with other linemen. According to the Union Agreement, there could only be one Apprentice to a crew, to avoid having multiple apprentices and not enough linemen. So, each Apprentice across the Division had experiences based on their local linemen and local work practices. We found out how inconsistent things were across the Macon Division when the apprentices came from the outside districts to the Macon Training Crew. To give you an example: a Quadruplex Service has three hot legs. One had a single marking, one had two markings and the third leg was slick, with no ridges at all. In Macon, the slick leg was the high leg in a Delta Bank, 212 Volts. In Hawkinsville District, the high leg was the leg with two markings/ridges. We all were getting it done but had our way of doing it!

TIMES WERE ABOUT TO CHANGE

J ust before I was selected for a Foreman's position, Clayton Byars
came to Key Street for Atlanta Corporate Distribution and asked for
some help. The company had decided a structured Lineman Develop
program was the way to go rather than having 6 different Region
Programs, the company would developpe a single program to be man-
aged by Klondike Training Center. He asked if I would write proce-
dures to be included in the new Lineman Development Program. I was
honored that they asked me to do that. I have been writing training
programs and re-writing safety rule books since then. Many companies
had to update their Safety Rule books and programs after the 2014
update to the 29 CFR 1910.269 Regulations.

The promotion to Crew Leader on the Training Crew in Macon
led to me being assigned as Crew Foreman of the Jonesboro District
Apprentice Training Crew. No one wanted to be the dedicated
Apprentice Trainer back in those days, so it was up to each Division
(and later, Region) to have their Apprentice Training Crew. This was an
issue because there was no structured, consistent program. Eventually,
this led to what we now know as Klondike Training Center. All the
training would be developed and presented at Klondike, by dedicated
Skills Trainers, for a consistent developmental lineman program. There
are many stories of the Apprentice Training Days in Macon, all good
experiences that I was lucky to be a part of. The fact that I was a Crew
Leader on the first Training Crew is a neat memory. One sad memory
is that shortly after I transferred to Jonesboro, my last "pole buddy",
Bruce Peterson, was diagnosed with cancer and later passed from it.

I still miss him today. "Tater" was a special guy. His family and mine were good friends and we were all sad to hear the bad news. Bruce showed up at the Macon Division golf tournament and surprised us. Even though he could not play, he wanted to see everyone. That was the last time I saw him.

More Memories

I look back on the stories I have told in this book and think of many more that I could have written down. I did not want the book to be as thick as Webster's Dictionary. My publisher suggested that I author another book about the remainder of my career at GPC and 15 years as a Safety Consultant to over two hundred customers, having traveled through and trained in all 50 states. I have been asked to testify in and deposed in 20-25 court cases. My largest customer had several thousand employees, and the smallest had 24 employees. I did my best to try and serve them all and provide the best training possible. I had up to eight employees for working some years, and Wayne Hardin worked with me for seven years as my I&I Instructor and Auditor.

When I was transferred to Jonesboro and moved to the Jonesboro/ Stockbridge area, it started an entirely different chapter of my life. I was no longer a Lineman, but a Supervisor, a Contractor Manager, a Field Safety for Metro South, and Atlanta Regions, and finally a Safety Consultant for all of Georgia Power's 9200 employees. That is another reason I retired early, left GPC, and started my own safety consulting business that is still operating today, 15 years later. I have many customers and friends asking me every day when I am going to retire. I tell them quickly that I love what I do, and if you love what you do, you never work. The stories of all those positions will be in the second edition, which will follow this book.

Author Notes

I have enjoyed recounting all these memories for this book. I have many friends and former co Workers to thank for helping me to remember the names of employees whom I haven't seen or heard from in 30 years or more. I truly thank all who assisted me. There are many more stories I could have included, but to keep the book from being too long, I could not have included them. Many names that I should have mentioned and did not. My career as Journeyman Linemen only prepared me for the next part of my career. I have been blessed and fortunate to have had the career and enjoy the life I have had. If you enjoyed this book, the next one will be just as entertaining and a joy to read if you are a lineman or in the utility industry. Thank you for purchasing the book and I look forward to writing the next one. A portion of the profits from this book will be donated to Joseph M. Still Burn Center in Augusta, Georgia to assist with the care and families of the victims burned by Electric Utility Systems. Again, thank you for your support.

CPSIA information can be obtained
at www.ICGtesting.com
Printed in the USA
BVHW071916140123
656241BV00007B/123

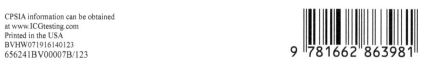